300

With My Best Wishes

To:

Rev. Donald Lomax

From:

Rev. Bert C. Pepper

1940

NON-VIOLENCE

IN AN AGGRESSIVE WORLD

NON-VIOLENCE
in an
AGGRESSIVE WORLD

by

A. J. MUSTE

Publishers

HARPER & BROTHERS
New York   London

This Book Is Dedicated

to my wife in gratitude for her loyalty and courage; and to the memory of certain of my college and theological seminary teachers—among them the late James G. Sutphen of Hope College, John H. Gillespie of the Theological Seminary of the Reformed Church in America at New Brunswick, New Jersey, and Arthur Cushman McGiffert of Union Theological Seminary. In the early years of the present century these men taught me Latin, New Testament Greek and Church History respectively; but since they were great teachers they taught me above all that the search for truth is endless and exciting, that the highest courage is to look truth straight in the eye, and that those who undertake to write or teach must utter the truth as they see it taking nothing away, adding nothing thereto, and in nought equivocating.

To strive to do this is to worship
the Lord thy God with
all thy mind.

Contents

I. RELIGION, REVOLUTION, AND DEMOCRACY   1

II. THE CROSS IN INDIVIDUAL LIFE   11

III. THE CROSS IN HISTORY   20

IV. THEORETICAL AND PRACTICAL DIFFICULTIES   30

V. PACIFISM AS REVOLUTIONARY STRATEGY—I   51

VI. PACIFISM AS REVOLUTIONARY STRATEGY—II   73

VII. DEMOCRACY, POLICE, AND PACIFISM   97

VIII. THE POLITICAL PROGRAM OF PACIFISM   132

IX. THE CHURCH AND THE REVOLUTION OF
PEACE   172

BIBLIOGRAPHY   204

INDEX   207

NON-VIOLENCE
IN AN AGGRESSIVE WORLD

Chapter I

Religion, Revolution and Democracy

THE ARGUMENT AND THE APPEAL OF THIS BOOK ARE ADDRESSED
TO THE PROTAGONISTS AND MEMBERS OF THREE GROUPS. MOST
Americans would agree that the future of civilization, as
we have known and cherished it, depends upon whether
the groups or movements to which I am referring survive
and achieve their basic aims. Each of them is today in a
critical situation, on the defensive rather than engaged in
a confident offensive, none too certain of survival, not to
mention victory, in this post-war world of ours.

The first group consists of the members and followers of
the churches, Christian and Jewish. The tradition out of
which these churches have grown, which in varied forms
they seek to express, and which they must adapt and apply
to the problems of the present age, has its roots in the books
of the Bible, the Old and the New Testament. Biblical
religion is Jewish-Christian prophetism.

The second group consists of workers and of intellectuals
more or less closely identified with the workers' movements, of trade unionists, Socialists, Communists, revolutionists. They are active in various degrees and ways in
the secular movement for economic and political change,
by reformist or revolutionary methods. This movement or

group of movements, in spite of its prevailingly secular aspect, derives its ideals, thoughts, and inspiration to a much greater degree than is often realized from the Jewish-Christian prophetic tradition.

The third group, which includes many individuals who also function in the other two, consists of those who believe in the democratic way of life and who are genuinely concerned about the adaptation of democratic concepts to modern needs and conditions. The democratic tradition also has its source to a much greater degree than many understand in the Jewish-Christian prophetic faith. For it was this faith that taught men the infinite value of the individual soul and that it befits each soul to bow the knee to God only and not, therefore, to any man. The God of Jewish-Christian prophetism is a creator, a worker, rather than an Absolute utterly removed from mundane affairs or a Mind engaged in dispassionate contemplation of them. "My Father worketh hitherto," said Jesus, "and I work." For Moses to meet this God meant meeting One who was as a "bush that burned and was not consumed," burned unceasingly because of the oppression wherewith the Egyptian bosses oppressed Israelitish laborers. For Moses to undergo the experience of receiving God into his soul meant that he must identify himself with these oppressed kinsmen of his and, as some one has put it, "organize them into Brickmakers' Union Number One and lead them in a walk-out from Egypt." The supreme incarnation of God and the greatest of the prophets of this Jewish-Christian faith was the Carpenter of Nazareth.

In modern times these movements of prophetic religion, social reform and revolution, and democracy have often been indifferent to each other and sometimes they have worked at cross purposes, not always without malice. There are growing numbers in each camp, however, who are seeing that the fate of each is largely bound up with that of the other two. For this the dictators and their régimes are largely responsible. They display an impartial hatred for the churches, the workers' movement (in Russia, no more than in Germany or Italy, are genuine labor unions, independent alike of employers and of the state, tolerated), and all liberal and democratic organizations and institutions. Once again men see through their tears what in quieter times unseeing eyes did not discern.

Organized religion, Jewish and Christian, stands or falls with a free labor movement. In the dictatorships of the Right or the Left, where there are no genuinely free organizations of the workers, there are presently no free churches either. Where liberties of speech, press, and assemblage are destroyed, freedom of worship does not survive.

The trade unions have generally had some awareness of the fact that their future is bound up with democracy, though their allegiance to the latter has too often been largely lip-service. Recently the radical political groups seeking social reform or revolution have in most cases also ceased their vitriolic attacks both on democracy and on religion, and have indeed declared that there was no essential incompatibility between their own aims and those of liberal and religious groups. The motivation has probably often been purely opportunistic, yet not always. As we shall have occasion to discuss at greater length later, however, the dependence of the whole movement for social change and of the cause of democracy on religion is a much more fundamental and crucial matter than most radicals and democrats have yet understood. The failure of the reform organizations, unions, and radical parties to make steady and substantial progress is due in a large number of instances to a simple lack of sound human material. Leaders and rank and filers lack the capacity for self-effacement, the freedom from the desire for ease and other more sordid desires, the self-discipline, the courage, often the common honesty and decency, without which a movement cannot maintain its own morale and present a united front to the enemy. The movements which set themselves the task of putting an end to injustice, inequality, and hate and building a brotherly world have lacked the spirit of brotherliness in their own ranks. They have had little or no concern about the moral and spiritual problems of developing sound human beings. They will come to still more grief unless they begin to take account of these moral and religious factors. They have been right in prophesying that men cannot live the good life under a "bad system"; but it was shallow to think that a "good system" under which men should automatically become good could be achieved, and still more shallow to think that the character of the men who worked for the new system and the means they employed were matters of no importance.

The problem of democracy which concerns so many in this country today is likewise in the last analysis a problem of the nature of the human being, the quality of the individual. If human beings are essentially animals, even though they be very complicated and clever animals, then every society, every state, every economic system, no matter how the fact may be temporarily camouflaged, will be essentially a wolf-pack with the strongest and most brutal of the wolves as the dictator; politics and business will be simply "the game of who gets what when"; and then the distant as well as the immediate future will be with the dictators, since they are in that case building on the realities of human nature. Only if the human being is a creation of spirit, a being capable of making moral decisions and therefore of governing himself, is the dream of a free democratic society capable of fulfillment. Long ago Edmund Burke stated the problem: "It is inevitable that a restraint be placed on human will and appetite somewhere, and the less there is within, the more there must be without: it is contrary to the eternal nature of things that men of intemperate minds should be free." Here again the Jewish-Christian prophetic life-view is of the utmost importance, for the concept of the dignity and moral responsibility of the individual has ever been one of the foundation stones of prophetic religion.

The concept of human dignity is, however, a religious one in the sense that it depends upon one's conception of the nature of the universe. Man is not self-sufficient. Obviously he did not create himself. He is the product or creation of something, Some One. Only, therefore, if men stand in a living relationship to God, to a Moral Reality beyond themselves, can they live a life of freedom and fellowship. "Only the belief in objective rational truths and moral values can preserve freedom; for it is only through the right of appeal to objective standards that men can judge the actions of their government and resist them when they believe them to be wrong. . . . If standards of right and of rationality vary in different societies, and are mere products of a social system, then the individual loses his right of appeal, the independence of his conscience is undermined, and he can be compelled to conform to whatever the state chooses to recommend." In the final analysis it is those and only those who bow the knee to God who do not bow the knee to any man.

Disaster consequently overtakes men and civilization when they lose a living contact with God. Men today consider it a childish thing, something educated and sophisticated people do not do, to bow the knee before God and to be "humble followers of the gentle Jesus." But the result is obviously not that they have become upstanding, free men who no longer bow the knee to anybody. They bow the knee before Hitler, Mussolini, Stalin, some political boss, some social arbiter or some other idol. Those nobler spirits who cannot bring themselves to do that, sink into disillusionment, if not cynicism, into that feeling of being able to see through everything and everybody and not being able to see anything in anything or anybody any more, which afflicts many of the most sensitive spirits of our time. This is an inexorable spiritual law which has been demonstrated in many historical periods: if men really come to believe that they are the highest beings in existence, that there is no moral reality beyond them, they do not for long trust or respect themselves or each other. The diplomacy of our day is a sufficient illustration of the point. Democracy cannot become a living and advancing faith in an age when it is so sore beset, unless we can recover our faith in man, and we cannot recover faith in man unless we recover faith in God.

In great measure, then, Jewish-Christian religion, social advance, and democracy stand or fall together. We need not devote much space to elaborating the point made at the very outset that all three of them face a crisis, are engaged in a not always successful defensive conflict, and are by no means assured of survival, except as the faith of persecuted minorities, in a world given over to secularized and brutalized religions, social rigidity and regimentation, and totalitarian political régimes. Even this may indeed be too bright a picture of the future of the western world which may be headed for the economic and political disintegration and cultural eclipse of another Dark Ages.

When a movement arrives at such a crisis, its followers have, broadly speaking, three courses open to them. One possibility is simply to continue repeating the old slogans and trying to carry out the old formulas—the beating of your head against a stone wall technique. Alike in the churches, the unions and the political parties, and in the liberal movements there are die-hards trying that course. Another possibility is to retire from the conflict into ivory towers of varied architecture, more or less sumptuously furnished. "Tired radicals," tired liberals, tired intellectuals, tired preachers, tired reformers, plenty of them are trying this ivory tower technique. The third and only hopeful possibility is to adopt a scientific approach, to be willing to look at the situation afresh, to revaluate one's aims, strategy, and tactics, and thus to find a solution adapted to the new situation. This scientific attitude is also the attitude of Jewish-Christian prophetic religion, it should be noted. Repentance is the gateway to salvation, and repentance means precisely to have your mind turned upside down, to get a new focus on everything. Further-more, the great prophets have always in effect said to Israel: "You must repent first, not the other fellow. It is not the devilish Egyptians, Babylonians, or Romans who are in the first instance to blame. You must not think that the tragic crisis in which you and the world find your-selves can be understood in terms of a battle between the angels and the devils, the good and the evil, the just and the unjust, those who are perfectly willing to listen to reason and those who don't understand anything except force—with, of course, you and your friends cast in the rôle of the angels, the good, the just, the reasonable! No, you must get over this romantic approach to great social issues. You must regard them as problems, objectively, realistically, freeing yourself from self-righteousness and self-importance."

A scientific attitude will guard us, of course, against the assumption that there is a panacea, an easy, pat formula, for ushering in a new world-order. It may well be, how-ever, that some one issue is at the given period the most basic and urgent. The Christian or prophetic conscience is often sensitive to the evil in some social institutions before men in general are aware of it. Those who share this sensitivity must bear witness to their concern. In the beginning and perhaps for a long time they will constitute a minority; it may be a despised and persecuted minority. A time comes, however, when such changes occur in the political and economic scene, such advances in the realm of culture, as to make the institution in question clearly unfit for survival. Then, after a more or less violent struggle on the part of its beneficiaries, or rather those who still delude themselves into thinking that any benefit may be derived from it, the institution is removed. Thenceforth the general conscience of mankind agrees in condemning it and would regard with horror any proposal to restore it. Something of the kind happened with the institution of chattel slavery, for example, within the memory of men still living.

Similarly, since the dawn of civilization there have been groups and individuals—they include such fixed and powerful stars in mankind's firmament as Lao-tse, Ikhnaton, Isaiah, Jeremiah, Jesus, St. Francis, George Fox, John Woolman, Gandhi, Kagawa—who have renounced war whether between nations or in social conflicts, have believed in a "spirit that taketh away the occasion of all wars," have advocated and employed non-violent methods to achieve justice and brotherhood.

I believe that we have now arrived at the stage when our whole technological, economic, political, cultural situation is such that the traditional attitude of, for example, the Society of Friends (Quakers) toward war must be universally adopted or mankind, and in particular European-American civilization, must suffer a colossal reverse. Whatever may have been the case in the past, there is no rational or moral justification left for war. To all followers of Christianity and of Judaism and of any worthy faith, to all who seek a social order embodying justice and fraternity, to all who cherish liberty and democracy, each day's developments cry out from the housetops what Jesus counseled long ago, what the Spirit has so often whispered in the inner chambers of man's soul: Renounce violence. Put up your sword into its place; for they that take the sword, no matter how great the provocation appears to be, no matter how fair the goal, no matter how certain the "victory," shall perish by the sword.

Religion, social progress, democracy depend for survival and triumph upon the adoption of a thorough-going, deeply motivated, positive, realistic pacifism.

Chapter II

The Cross in Individual Life

I AM A CHRISTIAN BELIEVER. I WAS BROUGHT UP IN THE CHRISTIAN CHURCH. AFTER SOME YEARS DURING WHICH I WAS a thorough-going Marxist-Leninist, renouncing all religion as "opiate of the people" and the church as nothing but a bulwark of a reactionary status quo, I returned to the church and to faith in the love of God as revealed in Jesus Christ as the one means of salvation for the individual and for mankind. I must find a sanction for my pacifism, therefore, in my Christian faith, and it is at this point that I naturally begin the argument.

The case for Christian pacifism does not rest upon proof-texts from the Bible. By that I do not mean that a careful study of the texts that appear to bear directly on the question of war and violence does not support the pacifist position. I believe it does. All Christians and students of the Bible ought to read that comprehensive and convincing book, *The New Testament Basis of Pacifism* by Professor G. H. C. MacGregor of Glasgow. It deals with all the pertinent passages.

Christian pacifism arises out of and is bound up with the very essence of the Christian world-view, the most precious and distinctive doctrines of our faith. Numerous answers have of course been given to the question: What is the essence of Christianity? Men who agree on the substance of the answer may vary greatly in the formulation of it. There is, however, a concept of the Christian message to which the Saints and the church in its great periods have constantly returned. When men have rejected it, it has been not so much because there was any question as to what Jesus and the New Testament were trying to say as because they did not dare face the moral implications and demands of the revelation. That concept of the Christian faith could be expressed somewhat as follows.

In the first place, the Christian religion has something to say about the nature of the universe, of God. Jesus put it in the simple and human terms which He constantly used, saying, "God is Father, God is Love." If this is more than a form of words, an incantation which gives us a comfortable feeling inside when we repeat it, it must mean that the most real thing in the universe, the most powerful, the most permanent is love. For God, "the creator of heaven and earth," is Love.

The doctrine of the Trinity itself suggests that according to the Christian view God cannot rightly be conceived in terms of a hard, enclosed, mathematical unity. You have to think in terms of relationship, of fellowship from eternity to eternity—of Eternal Father and Eternal Son and the Eternal Spirit of Love which grows out of the relationship between them.

It must follow that every human organization and institution will be able to endure and to function in the degree that this divine, creative element of love, of fellowship, is embodied in it and promoted by it. On the other hand, any institution—family, economic system, state, church—will fall to pieces in so far as it embodies fear, envy, domination, exploitation, strife, and not fellowship. "There is honor among thieves," it has been said. It is not always appreciated that there has to be even among thieves something of honor, of fellowship, of trust, of simple confidence of one human being in another which transcends considerations of immediate gain and safety, or it would be impossible for them to carry on their "business." The societies of thieves are so notoriously short-lived and precarious because there is so little fellowship in them, in which respect our political and business systems too often closely resemble them, and they also prove short-lived and precarious!

It follows also from this conception of God that the deepest reality, the most vital force always works quietly, unobtrusively, steadfastly, works through patience and gentleness and humility. God, life in its deepest sense, does not work through thunder, bluster, aggression, strife, whether that strife be labeled offense or defense. Even in the Old Testament this note is frequently sounded. Elijah, for example, had to learn that God was not in the earthquake, the wind, the fire. After all these came "a still, small voice," and that was God. God's people are told, "In quietness and confidence shall be your strength." Of the Messiah to be it is said that He will not quench the smoking flax or break the bruised reed.

Luke's account of the first Christmas represents the angelic choirs as proclaiming the same lesson: "There is born to you this day in the city of David a Savior which is Christ the Lord. And this shall be the sign unto you. [This is the proof that God has come at last to bring redemption.] Ye shall find a babe!" It is needless to recall all the utterances of Jesus which teach us to find power in the silent, gentle forces and beings. He saw this principle as basic in sub-human as well as human life. When He called on his disciples to trust this force of love, He pointed to the flowers: "Behold, the lilies of the field, how *they* grow; they toil not, neither do they spin [no fuss and fuming here] and yet I say unto you that even Solomon in all his glory [and frantic emulation of other Oriental monarchs] was not arrayed like one of these."

Jesus saw the principle operating also in human relationships: "You being evil know how to give good gifts to your children." In spite of all your struggling against the good, against love, you cannot get away from it. Paul called attention to the same fact about life in Corinthians 13. "Love never faileth." People think Paul was rhapsodizing, that the Bible is "idealistic," by which they mean it is not realistic. The fact is the Bible is starkly realistic. Has anyone ever found a "sob-story" in it? Paul is stating a fact, not a pious hope. Love never faileth. Human beings will express it in the most unlikely circumstances. They fall into it in spite of themselves as iron filings are drawn to a magnet. There is not a slum home, nor a gangster's hideout where you will not find some sudden manifestation of it. The soldier on the battlefield will give his last drop of water to a wounded comrade, aye to the wounded foe. It is a job to keep them from fraternizing in the trenches!

One recalls the phrases of the Irish mystic Æ about "the sudden gentleness that stays the blow—the kiss that foemen give pausing in battle—the tears that fall over the vanquished foe."

"Now abideth—love," and that "now" may mark a day of fiercest battle, of unspeakable calamity, of outrageous wickedness. It will still be true: Now abideth love, the love of man and maid, of parent and child, of friends, of former foes, and of man for a Reality beyond himself, in which for all its vastness and terror he has also discerned a likeness to himself and solicitude for him.

Anthropologists, psychologists, criminologists, and such, we may note in passing, are increasingly teaching what many a gentle saint through the ages has exemplified, viz., that it is this same method of gentleness, selflessness, non-aggression, fearlessness that is alone successful in the training of animals, in contacting primitive peoples, in the education of children, and in the treatment of criminals and the mentally sick. Those who have not already done so should read the delightful and endlessly stimulating writings of Gerald Heard on these matters.

Certainly the very heart of much of Jesus' teaching and life is found in such lines as those of Strickland Gillilan:

> The grass grows slowly up the hill
> With faith the torrent cannot kill
> And rocks are rough, and still the clover
> The stony field will yet run over—
> And I know nothing that the true,
> The good, the gentle cannot do.

Woodlands that the winters sadden
The leaves of Spring again will gladden
And so must life forever be—
The gentle hands work patiently
And yet accomplish more forever
Than these too strong or those too clever.

So toils an undiscouraged God
And covers barren fields with sod,
And so will hate and sin surrender
To faith still strong and love still tender—
And I know nothing that the true,
The good, the gentle cannot do.

It may well be that the gentle reader is beginning to feel
that the mood of the discussion is a bit over-gentle, idyllic,
even saccharine. The world, if you look at it squarely,
does not seem to be run on the basis of gentleness and love!
Surely there is opposition, hatred, sin? The Bible does not
evade that question. It may be said that the Bible deals just
with this fact of sin and not much else. And what does
God do about opposition and sin? Surely the answer of the
New Testament is clear and explicit on the point. God
does the only thing He can do, being the God revealed in
Jesus Christ, the Father. He keeps on loving the sinner.
He does not seek subjects or victims. He is Love and can
find no joy save in answering love. But love alone can
invoke love. God has no "wisdom" and no "power" save
the wisdom and power of a true Father in dealing with
His children.

But if you keep on loving in the face of rejection and

evil and sin, then you suffer. "While we were yet sinners God loved us." That means suffering. And that is why the Cross is the central mystery and the inevitable symbol of the Christian faith—the Cross that is graven on the very heart of God. At the foot of that Cross the Christian finds personal salvation. In the presence of such love as was manifested there, he learns to be desperately ashamed of himself and not to be ashamed of the tears of penitence.

> Mine, mine was the transgression,
> But thine the deadly pain.

But also he rises into newness of life, for if in the final analysis it is such love as this with which we have to deal, then all things are indeed possible, then it is possible for us "to be transformed into the same image from glory to glory."

Perhaps we should observe at this point, in order to guard against misunderstanding, that all this does not mean that the Christian view of sin and of redemption from it is an easy-going one. Quite the opposite. God's moral law is not suspended for men, because God desires sons made in His own image to love Him. Only by voluntary obedience to the divine standard can man achieve that status. And what the Cross says is that when man fails through sin, the price that must be paid by the divine love is beyond description. It can only be suggested to our human apprehension by the figure of God, who "spared not his own Son, but delivered Him up for us all." But the Cross says also that that is precisely what God did, that there was no other method save this of suffering love to redeem us, and that it is somehow in this divine drama of love that will not let men go that we are given our profoundest insight into the heart of God, the nature of the universe.

Obviously for the Christian, when it comes to his own dealings with evil in his fellows, all this poses the question: "If God's answer to evil is forgiveness of the evil-doer, is love which stops at no sacrifice for the sinner, then what must my answer be?" Nowhere in the New Testament do we find the slightest hint that while God uses one way to meet evil and redeem the sinner, the Christian or any human being is to use another method in dealing with his fellows. There are, on the contrary, the most explicit instructions that we are to be perfect as the Father in heaven who "makes His sun to rise on the evil and the good, and sends His rain on the just and the unjust." If "vengeance" is to be thought of at all, let it be left to God, says the Apostle, inferring that men who resort to vengeance sacrilegiously invade divine prerogatives.

Jesus was constantly reminding men, as had the greater prophets of the Old Testament, that in a situation where strife and tension exist, the responsibility rests not with one but with both or all parties involved. You must, therefore, take hold of the tension first at the point where you really can reach it, namely in yourself. You must realize that you have sinned, you have not had complete faith in the good, either. Therefore, you must repent, get a new focus on the situation and on yourself. "Take out first the beam that is in your own eye."

And what if even that does not stop and win over evil-doers? What if they reject and despise and fight Jesus himself, and us in those moments when we have really in some degree entered into the spirit of Christ? He who said:

"Let your yes be yes and your no, no," gives us here also a straightforward, unequivocal answer. He staked his life on it. The answer is, again, the Cross. If evil rises up in its final, least rational, least excusable, most hideous form, then accept suffering at its hands and on its behalf. Let it nail you to the cross. Take suffering into your own soul; do not drive its sword into the flesh or soul of an erring child of God. Thus you will be showing the power of Divine Love, for God is Love, to outlast and outwit all opposition; not even death can force it from its path. And there is no power to overcome evil, to break the heart of sin, like the power of suffering love, the Cross. "I, if I be lifted up, will draw all men unto me."

Can any Christian look back on the history of these nineteen centuries, down into his own heart, and deny that this is so? To do so would certainly require not merely a reinterpretation but a rewriting of the New Testament. So deeply indeed has the concept of the Cross been graven on our thinking that we habitually justify the man who goes to war on the ground that he is a Cross-bearer, one who is prepared to lay down his life for his fellows!

We are, however, frequently told that the method of suffering love is indeed applicable, and the only one the Christian is permitted to use, in personal relationships, but it cannot be applied in wider spheres of politics, economics, and relations between nations. We must next consider what the Jewish-Christian scriptures have to say on that point.

Chapter III

The Cross in History

SOMEONE HAS USED THE PHRASE, "THE CROSS AS MAKER AND YARDSTICK OF HISTORY." THAT SUGGESTS, FOR ONE THING, THAT it is on "the plane of history," not in a "beyond history," but in this history of men, classes, nations in which exploitation occurs and wars break out, that the Cross, the way of the Cross, is a force and an applicable standard of judgment. The phrase suggests also that it is on the great scale of history, in the affairs of races, classes, and nations, and not merely or chiefly in intimate relations between individuals, that the Cross is the determining force and conquering ideal and pronouncer of judgment—that it is history which validates the Cross.

Such ideas are, however, constantly challenged and the pacifist's espousal of them deprecated and scorned, both in and outside the church. The world has many maxims in which it conveys its wisdom in the matter to its children: "Business is business"; the dictum of the English statesman, "You can't handle the Irish question on the lines of the Sermon on the Mount"; and the older "God is on the side of the big battalions."

What is more important and serious for us is that in theological and religious circles also the implications of that phrase I have quoted are challenged. The problem of politics and economics, we are told, is that of justice, not love. "In the field of collective behavior the force of ego-istic passion is so strong" that nothing more than the provisional and precarious harmony of a balance of power can be achieved. Emil Brunner, in a familiar passage, warns that "the projection of ideal (political) programs is not only useless but harmful. . . . The prophetic demand, which does not concern itself with the possible and impos-sible, has, of course, its own relevance as proclamation of the unconditioned law. But it has this significance only if it is presented not as a specific program but as a general demand, i.e., if it does not involve immediate political realization."

But it seems to me that in the Jewish-Christian revela-tion the Cross is the crucial event in history, our human history; that the concept of the Cross, of suffering love as supreme redemptive power, was a social concept, which was revealed to men who faced overwhelming and bitter historico-political and economic dilemmas as a way of meeting precisely such dilemmas; that it is impossible to build up a scriptural-prophetic theology which does not demand the practice of love in all the relationships of life and promise the reign of God on earth.

The concept of God himself as One who suffers with peoples at a definite historical moment when they groan under quite concrete social oppression, and Who takes measures to redeem them from this bondage and to set up a kingdom based not on power but on ethical foundations, on a love (covenant) relationship between men and God and men and men—this is already prefigured and in part expressed at the very beginning of Jewish religious history. The record is found in the Book of Exodus which gets its name from a historic "walk-out" led by Moses.

But the idea becomes much clearer in later prophets. Israel began with a conception of God largely tribal. God is power. He is patron of your tribe and his law runs in its territory, not beyond. If you have might in relation to other tribes, it means your god is puissant. He is really your "blood" (Jewish or German), your might as tribe or nation, personified and idealized. If you are licked in battle, your god has been licked.

What ordinarily happened then was that your tribe was absorbed, if not annihilated, and you accepted the victorious god. But that did not happen to Israel, hemmed in and presently crushed like some Belgium or Czechoslovakia between the empires of Egypt and Mesopotamia. Israel survived its destruction as a nation. How? Why?

The only answer history gives is that in that crisis Israel through the prophets received and in a slight degree accepted a revelation of God, a deeper insight into the character of God, of ultimate reality. This revelation was proclaimed by the prophets to a nation caught in that definite historical situation, not, as Brunner would have it, as "unconditioned law," a merely "general demand," but for "immediate political realization."

The revelation came to this: God is not power, domination. This is not the final reality. The thing that counts is not a state which has power, economic, political, and military, as against other states. Righteousness, and again as in Exodus, "social righteousness," counts. But righteousness is not geographical in character. It reigns, if at all, everywhere—even in Egypt and Babylon of your captivity.

The prophets went a step further. Put it this way: If as a nation you suffer defeat and this does not prove that God is weak and therefore to be cast off, you still face the question of whether your suffering, the suffering of the righteous, of the chosen people, is a proof that God is unjust. If you believe that your suffering is basically unjustified, two things will happen. First, you will throw the blame on the other nation which "causes" your suffering. Second, you will presently give up trying to live righteously, for what is the use of following a God who inflicts boils precisely on Job? (The "inscrutability" of the ways of providence is a partial but not a final and complete answer to this problem.)

The answer of the great prophets was in substance: Righteousness is still righteousness. So far from being unjust, God loves and suffers for the unjust. Now, if that is your approach, you must first of all measure yourself against that righteousness and love. From that you reach the insight that you suffer, not because of the hellishness of these Egyptians or Babylonians, this sadistic dictator or that; you suffer because you have sinned, have exploited the poor, have tried to become a predatory military power yourself. Therefore you must repent, change yourself.

When you achieve this height of humility, you are, so to speak, taking sin on your own shoulders, your own heart. First of all it is your own sin, which you do not now try to project on the other fellow so that you may hate and slay him. But also, by rising to this higher moral position—of self-accusation, non-vengeance—your attitude toward the "enemy" undergoes a revolutionary change. It has become impossible for you to hate him with the implacable hatred of the self-righteous. Like yourself, though with more excuse, because he has not known the law as you have, he is caught in the toils of evil. Thus, as it were, you take on your soul the burden of the enemy's sin too, you suffer for him, you want him too to become the subject of Jehovah's law. You, Israel, become "the suffering servant of Jehovah," a redeeming agency, because you become like Him who loves sinful man and has a cross graven on his heart. "Pray for the peace of Babylon your great enemy!" cries King Zedekiah in Franz Werfel's novel *Hearken unto the Voice*; "Shall a man pray for the peace of his slayer who sets the sword to his breast?" Jeremiah replies, "I realize what I have done." Zedekiah cries, "And you do not shudder with horror at—at—the impossible?" Jeremiah bows his head: "The Lord demands of them and of us. . . ."

Let us turn now to consider Jesus' wrestling with the same problem that confronted the prophets of the great age. Any one who thinks of Jesus as a secular revolutionist, socialist, or communist is certainly mistaken. But it is quite as mistaken to think of Jesus as a Barthian who could make distinctions as to the sphere of life in which the law of love is fully operative. He, too, finds his nation ground under the heel of the dictator. Nothing seems to me clearer than that He applied the teachings which we sketched in the preceding chapter to the crucial political and social question of his day, that of the attitudes of his people toward the Roman oppressors, toward Cæsar and Cæsarism.

He knows himself called to be God's instrument to redeem his people, "to proclaim liberty to the captives."

But how to do it? Surely He must achieve influence, power? He must take "the kingdoms of the world and the glory of them?" Then He will be able to use his place and power to establish God's reign. If this means that He must stoop, "bow the knee" a little, surely that could not be helped. If the Messiah is not to base His policy primarily on meeting material needs (making bread out of stones) and if He is not to impose himself by magical means (leaping from the pinnacle of the Temple), then He must in some measure take men as He finds them, must be "practical" and "realistic," a little flexible as to the means He employs. But it was precisely this suggestion of compromise, the idea that evil might overcome evil, that He rejected most decisively. He rejected it as Satanic—"Get thee behind me, Satan"—that is, as contrary to His fundamental conception of God. The God whose Son He knew himself to be was not a heavenly potentate, a celestial general, but the prophets' God of righteousness and love. So his servant could not be an earthly Cæsar. He must be "the suffering servant of Jehovah."

If one rejects the method of domination and violence in order to overcome evil and establish the reign of good, what means can he then use? He can live the life of love. He can proclaim it to his fellows and urge them to adopt it. He can expose the hypocrisy of those who have power in Church and state and the evils of their rule. He can organize in peaceful ways to bring about a different order. If a man does all these things, he will meet opposition. If he refuses to fight back, he is likely to be defeated and killed. Jesus accepted that fact. He rejected the way of the sword and knew that He would therefore have to tread the way of the Cross. Peter could not understand that, but when he exclaimed that the Christ whom he had just confessed must not be crucified, Jesus again said, "Get thee behind me Satan!" The idea that there is another way than this of suffering love was for Him the last, most subtle, most Satanic temptation which assails the good man, the man eager to help his fellows. Jesus' other contemporaries did not understand Him at this point either. They stood at the foot of His cross and said: "Let him now come down from the cross, and we will believe on him"—that is to say: "He is good and great, He could be Messiah, our deliverer, but not in this unrealistic, fantastic fashion. Let Him now come down from the cross and—" But Jesus had made His decision.

To His people Jesus in effect said: "Do not hate the Romans; love your enemies. You think the Romans are oppressors, they conscript you, they take your cloaks, they 'rob widows' houses'? But so do you, Pharisees. You too have violated all the canons of social justice, all 'the weightier matters of the law.' And it is worse for you, because you had the light of the great prophets of the past to whom you like to build monuments, whereas the Romans did not. The real reason you do not want the Romans around is because you want to have a monopoly on robbing widows' houses, you do not like those who can teach you lessons in exploitation and cruelty. But the judgments of the Lord which are true and righteous altogether overtake such as you.

"If now you, the chosen people of God, do not repent, change your whole outlook and take first the beam out of your own eye, making yourselves true servants of light and righteousness, then how can we ever get out of this mess into a better world? If even God's people can only join the endless circle of meeting evil with evil, if the salt has lost its savor, its distinctiveness, wherewith shall it be salted?

"Furthermore, if you do not live up to your greater light, if you trample it under foot, how can you honestly claim that you represent more sacred values, a higher order than the Romans, which you must and may defend by any means at your disposal? If war comes under these circumstances, it will not be a war of light against darkness, God's hosts against Satan's. It will be a war of brute force against brute force; or more accurately of one misguided group of God's children called Jews against another misguided group of God's children called Romans.

"A new, distinctive force and technique must be introduced into the situation. Do you, therefore, prove yourselves the sons of the prophets, rather than the sons of those who killed the prophets. Do you repent; give up selfish, imperialist ambition; renounce every foolish intention to overcome evil with evil, to stop Cæsar with his own weapons. Do you devote yourselves to infusing a spiritual principle, the saving social principle of brotherhood, into this great politico-economic structure which men have succeeded in building and which has such great possibilities.

"Do you do that and by being thus willing to risk your own life as one power-state among many, you will save yourself. And you will save this civilization, this magnificent body which needs a soul. Cæsarism will not be able to stand against such faith, righteousness, and love. I shall then be King, a King of a new kind, 'meek and riding upon an ass.' You shall know the peace of God, not the uneasy truces of man.

"If you will not take this way of peace, if in self-righteousness and selfishness and fear, you bring yourself down to Cæsar's level, use his weapons, you will join Cæsar's representative presently in crucifying me. Then destruction will overtake you, 'there shall not be left here one stone upon another that shall not be torn down.' And since the salt that should have preserved this civilization will have proven savorless, this civilization also will degenerate and perish.

"But," Jesus concluded his religious-political manifesto to his people, "that will not be the end. You will not have defeated my Father-God. Into His hands I shall confidently commend my spirit, that spirit on which every enduring society will have to be built. After three days I shall rise again. You will see the Son of Man coming in his glory."

So the prophetic revelation comes each time in a profound political, social, cultural, spiritual crisis marked by the emergence of brute power and its deification. Each time the prophet urges the nation to take the course of repentance, non-violence, love of the enemy—to take suffering on itself, not to inflict or desire to inflict it on others. Each time the prophet proclaims God, the Spirit, as mightier than the dictator. "The Egyptians are men and not gods, and their horses are flesh and not spirit." How are you going to meet this horseflesh except with more and better horseflesh, this Nebuchadnezzar, Cæsar, Herod, except with a bigger and better dictator? No, says the prophet, spirit, spirit of God, righteousness, love is mightier. And in each case the prophet of realism and doom proclaims also the undying hope: the Kingdom of God is at hand.

What is the verdict of history upon this religious-political strategy? The Jews did survive—not the Amorites and Hittites, nor yet the Egyptian or Babylonian empires—and they survived because the Remnant at least responded to the prophetic revelation and centered Israel's life in an idea, in God, not in power. And has not Israel, precisely through "the Law and the prophets," been a savior of mankind?

As for Jesus, whom has history vindicated; the Jews and Greeks and Romans who saw the Roman Empire and civilization as real and victorious and the Cross as a stumbling-block and foolishness? Or Paul and the early Christians for whom Rome's schools and palaces and banks and tramping legions were already gone and dead, who exultantly preached Christ crucified, and saw and heard none but "the Lamb that is in the midst of the throne"—not bull or lion or dragon or ass, but the Lamb, symbol of gentleness, of seeming helplessness in the presence of evil, of sacrificial love, which is at the heart of all real power and the secret of every final victory in this universe? Thenceforth and until this moment, history has been stamped with the seal "Anno Domini."

Chapter IV

Theoretical and Practical Difficulties

BEFORE PROCEEDING TO DEAL WITH OTHER ASPECTS OF THE PROBLEM OF WAR AND VIOLENCE, IT WILL BE NECESSARY TO deal with certain widely-felt and often expressed difficulties in the practical application to personal and social relationships of this way of non-violence which, we have been contending, grows out of the Christian or Jewish-Christian view of life.

Sometimes the basis for these difficulties is primarily theological. Thus there are theologians who proclaim what is sometimes called a "theology of crisis," sometimes denominated as "neo-supernaturalism." To cherish any hope that the kingdom of God will be realized on earth as the meaning and culmination of history is held to be human presumption and utopianism. This world lies in sin and always will. Some day "Christ will return," God will intervene from without and "give" salvation, establish His Kingdom. In the meantime, there is little we can do about it, except trust and wait. Men must seek, of course, to express love in the more intimate personal relationships, but in economic and political life the state rules and is entitled to exact obedience. If it calls men to war, they must obey, and the idea that war can be eliminated is utopian. In my youth in the Middle West, I encountered precisely this world-view among the most obscurantist and dogmatic ultra-Calvinist sects. It is indeed interesting to encounter it now as an expression of sophistication.

Others base objections to Christian pacifism primarily on a philosophy of society and history closely related to the theological ideas just mentioned. "Moral man" always lives in "immoral society." If you had a nation of Christians you might ask them to renounce war and practice non-violence, but you cannot expect a nation of non-Christians to act according to the Sermon on the Mount. In the nature of the case there is something non-moral or even immoral about a corporation, an economic system, a nation or state. They rest on power and violence. They render an important service by establishing approximate justice among men, restraining evil-doers. A degree of order having thus been established, individuals and small groups may practice love behind the shelter of its protecting wall. But the state itself must maintain itself against other power-states, it cannot practice love and sacrifice itself. Christians as citizens of the state must also, therefore, compromise the love-ethic of the New Testament and on occasion participate in war, economic and military. The exponents of this viewpoint are also given to warning us against "utopian" expectations as to the course of history. "Fragmentary actualization of salvation" is possible in world-history, one of them asserts, "the power of concrete demonic forces," this or that evil, will or may be broken at certain points, but the idea that "in some future age the demonic as a whole will be destroyed is a religious utopianism."

Then there are, of course, many sincere individuals,

including those who are committed to the renunciation of war and to non-violence as a faith and way of life, whose difficulties are primarily ethical and practical. Is Christian pacifism, for example, compatible with any use of force under any circumstances? Must one be a Tolstoyan non-resistant? If we refuse to take part in war, must we also in order to be consistent practitioners of the Sermon on the Mount "give away all our goods to feed the poor"?

We shall deal briefly in this chapter, first, with some of the theoretical aspects and, secondly, with some of the practical aspects of these questions.

In the first place, a philosophy which sets limits to the realization of the kingdom of God on earth, to the banishment of social evils, to building economic and political life and international relations on the standards set forth by Jesus and the prophets, is bound in the long run to be defeatist in its effects. War will certainly not be eliminated unless men have faith that it can be, that there is another foundation than power-politics on which international relations can be built. If men become convinced that such an aim is utterly utopian, the effect is not likely to be a more "practical" attempt to humanize warfare, for example, but complete despair or cynicism resulting in that glorification of violence which we witness in the various totalitarian philosophies. Besides, in matters of this kind, if Christians are to strive only for that which seems entirely practical and feasible in a world which is far from Christian, they will not even achieve that which is practical and feasible; because what that is can never be determined until there is thrown into the scale that faith and devotion which is prepared to go on regardless of "results," prepared to face the Cross. Is any one, for example, able to tell in advance what governments which contend that they cannot unequivocally renounce war would find it possible to do if they were confronted by churches which, in obedience to Christ and in disregard of what governments might say or do, would completely sever all relations with the system of mass-slaughter for any cause?

To put it another way, the very "tension" in the moral life which is so forcibly, and to a large degree justly, emphasized by certain of the "crisis theologians," and without which men relapse to the animal level, exists only if the impossible demand of the Gospel is laid upon them. Otherwise, as Nils Ehrenstrom has well said, "the relationship between the Kingdom of Christ and the political sphere" becomes "a tension of static parallelism" and not "a tension of dynamic transformation."

The effect of the attitude we are discussing is, in the end, bound also to be reactionary. If the world cannot be organized on the basis of fellowship anyway, if social life cannot be brought under the rule of Christ, if the vision of the Kingdom becomes dim, acquiescence in the status quo becomes the attitude of the church, and where the church provides "no vision, the people perish." On the other hand, the prophetic preaching, including that of Jesus, presents indeed a realistic and fiercely denunciatory picture of what is, but couples that with the proclamation that the Kingdom of God, "the revolution" is at hand, and is therefore always genuinely revolutionary, though its means are not those of the professional revolutionist.

I am convinced that "the crisis theologians" radically misapprehend basic elements in Biblical prophetic religion.

According to their philosophy of history, for example, this history, in which you and I live, in which Hitler and Stalin rape Poland, and Gandhi practices non-violence, is simply the re-enactment for an indefinite number of times of the drama of conflict between the demonic and the divine. It consists of cycles that return upon themselves. It has no goal. There have been philosophers, of course, who held such a conception. There is not the slightest warrant for it in Jewish-Christian prophetism. In prophetism history has a goal: God's reign of justice, fraternity, and peace.

It is said that the apocalyptic element in the teaching of Jesus shows that Jesus did not really expect His followers by ethical, social effort to strive for and achieve the Kingdom of God on earth—and by inference the elimination of such evils as war—but that the Kingdom would at "the end of the age" be "brought" from without by God or His Messiah. Certainly no one saw more clearly than Jesus that all power to serve God and to realize His will on earth comes from God by grace. But to represent Him as believing that God acts upon man in a non-moral, mechanical fashion from without, that God imposes Himself by force on men and on history, is to deny the most basic and distinctive element in Jesus' teaching. God is Father. God is Love. He cannot deny Himself, He cannot act otherwise than as a Father dealing with His children. Therefore, Jesus when He realized that He was God's Son, rejected the materialistic "supernaturalism" involved in the concept of a Messiah, a vicegerent of God, who made stones into bread and jumped from temple-pinnacles. It is impossible to conceive of Him as a coherent personality at all if we suppose that He after all expected that it was by the intervention of just such a magic-mongering Messiah that the Kingdom was in the end to come. Professor John MacMurray correctly points out in his book, *The Clue to History*, that "Jesus taught the means through which the establishment of the Kingdom of God in this world is to be achieved," means which were not Cæsar's, and that the apocalyptic element in His teaching is His "affirmation of the inevitability of its achievement." God wills the coming of His reign among men. He will not cease His struggle to win men by His love to the way of love. All their efforts to build society on any other basis than fellowship are doomed to fail. Because they are His children and He will not let them go, they will at last join Him in building the Kingdom, the divine-human society.

It is important to emphasize this point which Professor MacMurray expounds brilliantly in the book already referred to, viz., that the arguments against which we have been contending arise from a fundamentally non-religious, non-prophetic dualism which assumes that when Jesus talked about love and meekness, He was setting forth impractical ideals. "Love is, as a matter of fact, the basis of all human community." Speaking of the command to love your enemy, "the force of this conception will be missed if it is conceived as defining an ideal. Its justification is practical." What it does, to use another of MacMurray's phrases, is to take account of "the structure of reality." That structure is such that any society, any human order, goes to pieces precisely in the degree that it is not based on community.

Not because of His idealism but because of His realism,

MacMurray goes on to point out, Jesus rejected the temptation to overcome Cæsar by Cæsar's method and to achieve
the reign of God on earth by violence. To have yielded to
the temptation would have involved "a thorough-going
dualism between means and end." And if one had thus "to
act upon a principle which negated the religious principle
in order to reach the point at which the religious principle
could be put into practice," establish justice by violence,
in order that love might have a chance to function a little
in a sheltered corner, "the integrity of the religious consciousness" would be utterly destroyed.

Just here is the real source of that "tension" which
characterizes the utterances of some theologians. The heart,
if not the intellect, discerns that to accept war, reluctantly,
of course, and as a last resort, is to give up "the religious
principle." It is to admit that in this world the real power
is not the God and Father of our Lord Jesus Christ who
meets sin with suffering love, but Satan. God's reign is in
heaven, "beyond history," among "the dead." This is to
lose and deny the living, prophetic, God who is "the God
of the living." It is to fall into the absurd and blasphemous
notion that when it comes to the petty tyrants and the
mild sinners whom we encounter in our daily intercourse
in our homes and neighborhoods and churches, we can
afford to trust God and practice gentleness and love, but
when it comes to really big powers like Nebuchadnezzar
and Tiberius Cæsar and Hitler and Stalin, then we must
have something more substantial than "mere spirit" to
defend us, then it is a question of having bigger battalions
and achieving more killings and destruction than the
enemy!

We must now turn to the practical, ethical problems which arise when we question the validity of the way of the Cross in political and economic struggle. When a man says in effect that love is the true standard for individual and social action, but that in the given case it will not work, or that in the given case fidelity to the basic principle of love involves the use of means which are "far from ideal," he has, of course, by no means solved his problem. He has simply stated the problem as it appears to him. The question now is: If we may condone the fact that we ourselves and others live by some other standard than that of the love-ethic of the New Testament, what is that other standard? To admit, eagerly and in all humility, that we do not meet the Gospel standard and are therefore sinful men, is one thing. To conclude that we may, therefore, in a given situation, use another standard, is a totally different thing. By what standard is our compromising to be measured and kept from being too "realistic"? Just what is the workable compromise between the prophets and Machiavelli?

We do not wish for a moment to suggest that in relation to such problems as war or participation in the industrial struggle the task of living by the Christian law of love in an un-Christian world is for anybody a simple one. Christian pacifists have nothing to gain from minimizing the difficulties and seeking to over-simplify the problem. They must avoid giving the impression that they think they have an easy, cut-and-dried solution, for the problem of Czecho-Slovakia, Spain, China, Poland. Their critics sometimes unreasonably demand that pacifists shall be patent-medicine vendors, magicians, as it were. Men and nations go on for generations in utter disregard of Christian or pacifist counsels, and then, when a crisis develops, people turn upon the pacifist, figuratively hold a gun to his head, and demand: "Now how would you pacifists stop this thing?"—in five minutes and painlessly. But pacifists have sometimes perhaps fallen into a way of speaking which leaves them open to such attacks, using even so sacred and valid a phrase as "the way of the Cross" as if it were indeed a magic formula.

As this very phrase, "the way of the Cross" suggests, the idea that there is an easy and painless solution to great social problems is directly contrary to the very essence of the Christian pacifist position. There is always the Cross. The question is not whether in a sinful world there will or will not be suffering, but only whether we shall inflict suffering in the attempt to stop the evil-doer or accept suffering at the hands and on behalf of the sinner.

Similarly, pacifists must be prepared to admit that the course they propose may lead to failure and defeat—temporary, provisional failure, at least, but defeat as abysmal as that of the Cross seemed to be and in a real sense was. The question, again, is not whether defeat can always be avoided, but whether it shall be such a "defeat" as Jesus suffered on Calvary, or such a defeat as He might have met if He had yielded to the temptation to accept the conventional idea of the rôle of Messiah and sought to overcome Cæsar by Cæsar's methods.

Having said this, it is legitimate to go on to observe that the problem of compromise, the question as to whether the Christian can fulfill the law of Christ, and how this is to be done in a world which owns another Lord, is not peculiarly a problem for the pacifist. Every Christian faces such issues. It would not be difficult to show that every person who accepts a morality which is something more than a "higher expediency" faces them. In determining what in a concrete situation we must and must not do, we believe that we must submit ourselves to a twofold test. One is inner and has to do with our motives and purposes; the other is outer and has to do with the results of our actions and lives.

As to the first, the Christian, whether pacifist or non-pacifist, has given his allegiance to God revealed in Christ. He must give himself to a life of love such as that manifested in Jesus, that love of which William Law in his *Serious Call* remarks: "It is not Christian love, till it is love of all." Under no circumstances may he swerve from the inner commitment to obey Christ's law. Unless the Christian holds that standard before him, there vanishes from his life that very tension which, rightly enough, certain theologians emphasize as characteristic of the Christian life in an un-Christian world. In some sense, furthermore, and on many occasions, the Christian must remain true to his inner allegiance to this way of love even when there seems no practical justification for it, when the world will regard him as "romantic and utopian," when his course can only lead to the Cross, i.e., to humiliation and defeat. To all protests he will have to reply: "Thus far I go with you but no further; so help me God, I can do no other."

Wherever the Christian conscience may draw that line, it will be easy for some bright fellow to come along and show that there are logical flaws in the position and even that it is an absurd one. You can put the Christian in a logical corner and say: "Unless you give away all your goods to feed the poor and extricate yourself completely from our evil and un-Christian economic order, you may as well run or work in a saloon or distillery or a plant to manufacture poison gas or even perhaps a house of prostitution since these are inevitable parts of our economic system and if you stay in it at all you are 'involved' in them." You can say to the pacifist that if he will not make war against Hitler and believes that we must use the method of suffering love in dealing with him, then he has no business to use force to restrain any evil-doer at any time. You can perform mental acrobatics and argue that if the pacifist does any kind of work at all in war-time and submits to any kind of rules even in jail, he is releasing some one, if only an extra prison guard, for military service, and since he is thus "involved" anyway, he may as well submit to conscription and do anything the government orders. Or, contrariwise, you may argue that if he refuses to obey any orders and goes on a hunger-strike, he may simply be committing the sin of suicide rather than nobly laying down his life for Christ.

The same kind of dilemmas, however, can be put up to the non-pacifist Christian, or for that matter any ethical non-pacifist. When he takes his stand beyond which he in turn will not compromise, then there will be representatives of the Gestapo or the Cheka or the Intelligence Service, there will be psychologists and probably also Christian ministers on hand to tell him that he is acting on irrational grounds, that he is being emotional and impractical, and that he will fail in achieving his purpose by not going the full way. There will be some one on hand to tell him:

"Since you believed it right and Christian to bring economic pressure to bear on gangster nations, though this might involve starvation and misery for their peoples, you ought not now, since these measures have proved insufficient and these nations are now making or threatening war, to be squeamish about having your country go to war for the sake of democracy and to cure these people of their addiction to dictatorships." When he has accepted that argument, there will be some one on hand to point out that there is after all no clear line between combatant and non-combatant service; that any one who will fight in a trench should also be willing to fly a bombing plane which might kill women and children, or even, as the risk of an enemy victory develops, that it may be better deliberately to bomb some women and children and thus "save civilization"; and that since it is quite sentimental to think you can wage war without spies, he ought to turn spy for his country, his very reputation as a good and pious man giving him exceptional opportunities for such service. So things went in the last war, and who will deny that the cynicism and the addiction to the use of "impure means" thus bred in an entire generation resulted in grave injury to civilization and to the name and cause of Christ and the church?

If such dilemmas are pointed out not as an exercise in breath-taking swings on a flying trapeze but in a sincere spirit, this may be exceedingly useful. It will serve to remind pacifist and non-pacifist alike that we all live under the limitations of our heredity and surroundings and are apt to have much more sensitive consciences at some points than at others; that the moral life is infinitely complex and we must be on our guard against feeling self-righteous, complacent, or superior; and that we cannot extricate ourselves from involvement in our economic and social world and from sharing in the guilt of its failings and sins. But none of these things change one whit the standard by which we must judge ourselves and to which we must seek to conform. The command is still, "Be ye therefore perfect"; and as if to make sure there would be no misunderstanding Jesus adds the phrase, "as your heavenly Father is perfect." We must always be true to the motive of absolute love. "What we ought to do always is whatever is absolutely the best possible."

The non-pacifist is apt to take refuge in some form of dualism: love is the ideal, but you have to live by something less than the ideal in the real world; or love is the standard in personal relationships, but the command of the state is the standard in larger affairs such as war. The pacifist, however, may also seek escape in some form of dualism. He may claim that the voice of Christ in his soul commands him to do this and to refrain from that, and that therefore he need assume no responsibility for the consequences of his action. Over against any such attitude we must affirm that just as the non-pacifist is not exempt from facing the problem of inner allegiance to the command of love, so the pacifist is not excused by the fact that he is obeying that inner voice in renouncing war from submitting his actions, humbly along with his fellows, to the test and criticism of events, to political as well as to ethical and religious tests. Men may be deceived as to their real motives, they are indeed certain to be deceived if they are not willing to submit their ideas and ideals to the test of the actual results on the lives of those about them.

In this realm we find, again, that pacifist and non-pacifist are confronted with a common limitation and problem. We do not know all the consequences of our actions, today and in the future, in complex political and social situations. When, therefore, we say that we must test our actions by their results, we can only mean those results that we can foresee and calculate. If I am told that if I favor an embargo on the export of arms from the United States to belligerents I may be withholding a certain measure of support from Great Britain and France and thus may contribute unwillingly to results that I cannot foresee and might not desire, I readily admit that this may be true, in other words, that I am neither omnipotent nor omniscient, and that I have to leave something to God after all! But I am entitled to remind my non-pacifist brethren that when they propose to intervene in a war by furnishing munitions to one side, which may and probably will lead to sending men to help that side, they too are helping to release forces which they are utterly unable to control, whose consequences they cannot foresee, and over which, if the aftermath of the last war be any criterion, they will one day bitterly grieve.

Let us now for a moment apply our twofold criterion to the problem of war-renunciation. First, as to inner motivation, is it possible to wage modern totalitarian war, to do the things that must be done and refrain from doing the things that may not be done in the successful conduct of such war, and maintain the spirit of love, the presence of Christ, alive, sensitive, and active in the soul? Without passing judgment upon any individual, and freely recognizing that within the church today the "full fellowship of the Body of Christ" must be maintained between those who renounce war and those who are conscientiously led to participate in it, I feel that it is undoubtedly the case that the overwhelming majority of military experts, of rank and file soldiers, of modern youth, join with the Christian pacifist in replying to that question in the negative. Their sentiment is that of the youth in Charles Badger Clark's poem: "My father could mix his prayers and his shooting, and he was a right good man in his generation. Now I'm not so bad in mine, I reckon; but if I should pray like him I'd spoil it by laughing!"

What about the test of results, the political test? Every argument advanced against war-renunciation and disarmament, including unilateral disarmament, proves on careful analysis to be based on lack of realism, on a romanticism which simply fails to read and face the facts. The militarist and his puppet, the so-called man on the street, are each realists in their way about the brutal and pagan war-business. They recognize that war is—war; and that men and nations have to make up their minds either to renounce war altogether, or otherwise to accept and prepare for war—not imaginary, made-to-order, moderate war, but modern totalitarian war with modern weapons. The pacifist who believes the world is God's world and that only God's methods will work in it, also seems to me to be a realist, indeed the supreme realist. It is the theologians who think there is today a middle ground, who persistently refuse to face the facts, who insist that we must be realists, but themselves fall prey to most romantic notions about modern war.

A typical recent criticism of the practical application of Christian pacifism in the present crisis, by one who fully shares the spirit of such pacifism, made the following points: Though Christians as such must do as the Quakers and F.O.R., they must not urge their governments to take this way. "National disarmament, unreadiness to use any form of force in international relations, are more likely to involve a nation in shameful betrayal and moral cowardice than to enable it to express a truly Christian attitude—as Great Britain has recently been discovering." Under present conditions war cannot be avoided "unless peace-loving nations are willing to use coercive methods, 'stronger than words but short of war' against persistently aggressive nations." Christians "must not oppose their government in its attempt to parry the thrust of aggression by the only means now available."

The trouble with this argument is in the realm of politics, not of Christian ethics or casuistry, and the pacifist can, it seems to me, meet it fully and decisively on its own real ground. The line-up in the world today is read in terms of "peace-loving" versus "persistently aggressive" nations. That is superficial and misleading. It is the same reading that brought us disaster twenty years ago. The real line-up is between satiated powers determined to hang on to the 85 per cent of the earth's vital resources which they control, even if that means plunging the world into another war, and another set of powers equally determined to change the imperialist status quo even if that means plunging the world into another war.

For lack of arms Great Britain got involved in "shameful betrayal and moral cowardice"—presumably at Munich.

Read it deeply and realistically enough, and post-war history will tell you that Hitler was able to come to power in Germany at the moment when Great Britain and France wrecked the disarmament conference. It was there that the "shameful betrayal" of their pledged word and "moral cowardice" took place. And is British armament enabling the Chamberlain government, Czecho-Slovakia having been sold down the river, to pursue a Christian course now in defending as vital to peace, democracy, and civilization the Polish, Turkish, Greek, and Rumanian dictatorships? And in assiduously seeking an alliance with Mussolini?

Our reliance for Christian action in the international scene must now be, we are told, on "coercive methods short of war," i.e., on economic pressure. But it was economic pressure that brought the German people to the point where they accepted Hitlerism. These coercive measures stop "short of war" because, as Senator Pittman put it, "Why shoot a man if you can starve him to death?" But if you threaten to starve men and nations to death, you dare them to shoot their way out. Thus you have fooled yourself about stopping "short of war."

That is, of course, why even devout Christians and "pacifists-at-heart" never urge these "coercive measures short of war" and disarmament in the same breath, and why realistic "sanctionists," on the other hand, always couple proposals for such measures, which are advertised as a substitute for war, "just as good" so far as results are concerned but much cheaper and pleasanter to administer, with proposals for huge increases in armament. Why not disarm if these coercive methods short of war constitute so sovereign a remedy against "aggression"? But if it would

not be safe and Christian to disarm, then how much armament shall we as Christian citizens agree to? Enough presumably so that if the dictator and his people, refusing to
submit to the threat of starvation, "attack" us, we can
shoot them down. And then military experts will arrive
on the scene to remind us that in war an offensive is often
the best and "most merciful" defense. Other nations will
not believe that you will not take that offensive if you
have a chance. Then you have an armament race, international tension, and all the other preliminaries to—what
but world war?

Jesus proposed to his people the complete renunciation
of any idea of meeting Cæsar with Cæsar's weapons. They
were not "morally prepared" to take such a position.
Should Jesus then as a citizen have proposed something
else, though as a Prophet and Son of God he could believe
only in methods consonant with the spirit of the "suffering
servant of Jehovah"? But any other course, in the conditions of that day, meant destruction for his people, not
only physical but spiritual.

The United States is not ready for disarmament and
war-renunciation. What then shall we propose? A little
war-preparation, purely defensive preparation, refined economic warfare which can be safely waged at a distance
against supposedly sinful nations? Surely the alternatives
suggested are not living alternatives at all (such as moderate war-preparations in this day!), or they are alternatives which lead straight to disaster.

Much the same analysis may be made of the notion that
one may reject Lenin's view of the rôle of violence in the
class struggle, and yet not renounce violence altogether.

Lenin was passionately concerned about the fulfillment of the ancient prophetic dream of a world free from exploitation, injustice, and strife. But he held that you had to be "realistic" and that in the world as actually constituted no ruling class would yield its power voluntarily. The issue would have to be settled by the sword, and the working-class would therefore have to use dictatorship, terror, and repression, and be hard-boiled about it. As we shall have occasion to point out at length in a subsequent chapter, there is sense in saying that the Russian experience has taught that this course does not lead to the achievement of the goal of a better order, and that violence must be resolutely renounced by the advocate of social change. But to try to steer a middle course is to suppose that you can have a revolution under the rules and the supervision of the State Boxing Commission, a gentlemanly dictatorship and a benevolent Cheka. Any kindergartner in the revolutionary movement can point out that if violence is going to enter as a real factor in the situation, you must prepare for it, you must have as much of it as may be necessary to gain the decision, you must accustom the proletariat to the idea that in the show-down they must fight, you must arm them as the crisis approaches, you must take the offensive if that seems the best defense. In this field also, then, we are forced to conclude that in the world today we must choose between suicidal war with our modern enginery of destruction, or a clear-cut renunciation of war.

It is interesting to note that this conclusion is supported today by important persons and groups who deny that they are pacifists, at any rate in any "absolutist" sense. Thus the Roman Catholic church has contended that there are conditions under which a war may be "just" and participation in it a duty for the Christian. These conditions, as found in the writings of St. Augustine, the Thomists, and Francis de Victoria, are commonly stated as follows:

1. Gross injustice on the part of one, and only one of the contending parties.

2. Gross *formal* moral guilt on one side—material wrong is not sufficient.

3. Undoubted knowledge of this guilt.

4. Declaration of war only after every means to prevent it has failed.

5. Proportionate meting out of guilt and punishment. Punishment exceeding the measure of guilt is unjust and not to be allowed.

6. Moral certainty that the side of justice will win.

7. Right intention to further what is good by the war and to shun what is evil.

8. Right conduct of war—restraint within the limits of justice and love.

9. Avoidance of unnecessary upheaval of countries not immediately concerned and of the Christian community.

10. Declaration of war by lawful authorized authority exercised in the name of God.

An increasing number of devout Catholics, some of them organized in the PAX movement, contend that no conceivable modern war can fulfill these conditions. Accordingly they conclude that in our age good Roman Catholics should be conscientious objectors to war and refuse to participate in it.

In somewhat the same fashion the great Swiss Protestant

theologian, Emil Brunner, in his exhaustive ethical treatise, *The Divine Imperative*, concludes that "war has now become a method which cannot any longer be reckoned as an item in any political reckoning of gain or loss. The idea of 'winning a war' . . . no longer has any place in reality. . . . Therefore, if a nation were to disarm, and render itself 'defenceless'—in the old sense of the word—in order to prepare the way for the new form of 'security,' such action would not be a sign of political folly but of political wisdom, since it would demonstrate the possibility of a new way of political action. Again, when conscientious and politically sane citizens refuse to render a service to the state which used to be considered a very real service, but has now, in their opinion become politically useless, they show political wisdom. . . . They will bear witness to this new point of view [of the war-resister] by taking without complaint the punishment imposed upon them by the State, knowing well that the State does not yet see what they see."

A moment ago we alluded to the Leninist theory of the role of violence in the class-struggle. We must now turn from the discussion of the religious and Christian viewpoint on violence and non-violence to a more thorough examination of the problem of violence and war as it presents itself to the revolutionist and others interested in social change and progress.

Chapter V

Pacifism as Revolutionary Strategy

THE ORTHODOX MARXIST-LENINIST FORMULA AS TO HOW A NEW SOCIAL ORDER IS TO BE ACHIEVED RUNS AS FOLLOWS: "War is an inevitable accompaniment and outgrowth of capitalism; large-scale war, of capitalism in its present imperialist stage of development. There can be and is, therefore, no genuine struggle to abolish war apart from the struggle to abolish capitalism. Pacifists who want to abolish war but keep capitalism are sentimentalists when not downright dishonest. These wars," the argument continues, "over markets, colonies, fields for investment, help to disintegrate the economic and political structure. Furthermore, a moment arrives when the sufferings of the masses from economic disorganization and war become so intense that they can no longer bear them; they will then turn their guns upon their officers and the capitalists whom they represent; imperialist war will be transformed into civil war. Thus the proletariat will seize the reins of government, set up a dictatorship, and begin to lay the foundations of a socialist economy."

No one who has a modicum of education will argue that this formula as to how we are to get a new world, represents a "law" in the sense that the law of gravitation is a law or that two parts of hydrogen and one of oxygen always make water. In the realm· of history and social life we do not yet have such "laws." This generalization about social processes is based upon two lines of thought—first, upon tracing uniformities between the past and present and concluding therefrom that today certain causes are likely to produce certain effects; secondly, upon an attempt to estimate the economic and political factors in the present world-situation, and forecast the outcome.

As to the first line of argument, since no controlled experimentation is possible in this field and we do not know all the factors which operated in the past, it amounts to an argument from analogy. We know that the presentation of this argument is liable to dangers which must be guarded against. To what then does this argument, when brought to bear upon the problem of war and social change in the modern world, come? That in the past basic economic and political changes have been accompanied by violence and war and that they can only be achieved in the same way today.

Very likely we exaggerate the rôle played by violence in achieving the transition from feudalism, for example, to capitalism. The less obvious and dramatic changes in technology and in people's ways of thinking may have played a much more significant part. We may observe in passing that the practice of writing general history in terms of battles and wars is now outmoded and regarded as very superficial. The idea that the history of social revolutions must be written chiefly in terms of violence and coups d'état still lingers in many circles, both conservative and radical! Granted, however, that wars, civil and between states, have been one of the phenomena associated in the past with changes from one economy to another.

Over against the presumption that violence may therefore play a necessary part in such change today and lead to a new order, we may present an impressive array of instances—an array in which to my knowledge no exception occurs—of one civilization after another passing from an agricultural and feudal economy to one based largely on commerce and industry, dominated by the middle class, achieving a measure of democracy and imposing economic, political, and cultural institutions, producing great works of art, and then lapsing into a series of wars, after which came not a more advanced economy and a higher civilization, but general disorganization following upon the wastage of economic and human resources, and a return to barbarism.

If at this point the contention is advanced that we now have the machine and science and that consequently we need not expect the same cycle as before, then we are on the ground of the second argument, namely that the best estimate we can make of the forces operating in the world today leads to the conclusion that desired social change can only be achieved by the Marxist-Leninist method.

A few years ago a great number of people would have said that the case had indeed been proved and would have pointed to Russia for substantiation. "There," they said, "the job has been done, and nowhere else. It was done with the Leninist strategy which accepted violence, not as desirable, but as forced upon the workers by a ruling class that would not yield its power peaceably. The same strategy will produce the same result in other lands."

Today, none except the most extreme partisans or persons talking "for public consumption" will contend that the case has been finally proved. Certainly socialism has not been fully established in the Soviet Union. By definition, if that were the case, the state would have withered away, all remnants of class division would have been wiped out, and an unprecedentedly high standard of living would have been achieved. It is not even clear that development in the Soviet Union is today moving definitely and unmistakably in that direction. The state is not becoming less authoritarian, the dictatorship is not really being relaxed, despite surface appearances, and there appears a tendency to create privileged groups in the membership of the Communist party, the Red Army, the Stakhanoffites (more efficient piece-workers), and the farmers on the more fertile and favorably situated collective farms. Whatever be the interpretation of the executions of leaders in all departments of activity which have marked recent years, no one can plausibly argue that they demonstrate that the régime is and feels itself to be perfectly secure. In any case, the most enthusiastic exponents of the Soviet régime declare that all may be lost if war comes. Any compromises necessary to stave off war are therefore justified. As a result the Soviet Union now depends for its security on conventional military forces and upon military alliances with capitalist nations—devices which have meant insecurity rather than security in the past.

Since these words were first written, the astounding change in Soviet foreign policy from the line of the Franco-Soviet pact and the rapprochement with "the democratic nations" in order to "stop the menace of fascism" to the line of the German-Russian pact has taken place. On the possible or probable significance of this for the outcome of the European war we shall comment later. It is sufficient for the purposes of the present chapter to point out the obvious, viz., that this turn in Russian policy is further evidence that no such thing as a free co-operative commonwealth has been achieved in Russia and that this nation is being drawn the same as others into the dreaded vortex of war.

At this point we may observe furthermore that the post-war history of the labor and the revolutionary movement as a whole has by no means been one of steady advance, so that the philosophy and strategy with which it has been operating might be considered vindicated. On the contrary, the story is one of frequent defeats, much confusion and a shift from a confident offensive to a none too hopeful defensive, which would seem to call for a revaluation of philosophy and strategy.

If we turn now to ask what, using the best means of analysis and calculation at our disposal, we may expect to be the outcome of another general war, indeed of a series of imperialist wars and civil wars, fought under modern conditions and with modern weapons, then it seems to me one must be a romanticist, capable of flying in the face of all the evidence, of believing that two times two made four in 1918 but will make forty in 1938, in order to believe that such wars will open the gateway to socialism or a higher stage of civilization or a Christian society, or whatever term one may wish to use. It seems beyond reasonable doubt that the result is bound to be that the clock will be set back for generations, if not for centuries, that war will once more undo the results of centuries of human effort.

Nor, as I have already mentioned, does it seem to me that there is any escape from this conclusion in the reasoning of those who recognize that mistakes have been made in connection with the Russian developments and by the secular revolutionary movement in other lands, but who nevertheless believe that war and organized violence cannot be altogether renounced. Underlying such reasoning is the assumption that it is somehow possible to have a mild, little war, a nice, benevolent dictatorship, a gentlemanly revolutionary tribunal. There are no such animals left alive. The moment we admit that violence may have to enter into our calculations and may settle the issue, any tyro in the army or in the revolutionary movement can tell us that then you have to prepare your armament, and that furthermore an offense may be the best defensive. You are caught up, that is to say, in the full stream of militarism, whether it be capitalist or revolutionary.

If, then, we must depend upon the process of war and dictatorship to bring about a better social order, in line with the conventional Leninist formula, there is grave reason to think that we are reduced to despair. That something of this sort is indeed coming to be felt in Socialist and Communist circles is strikingly illustrated in a conversation which Ludwig Lore reported in the *Nation* some months ago. He asked S. Grumbach, Socialist vice-chairman of the Committee on Foreign Affairs of the French Chamber of Deputies: "Do you believe that another European war will end in a social revolution?" The answer was: "I no longer speak or think in terms of social revolution in connection with these questions. One does not work out plans for a castle in Spain when the roof is burning over one's head." But, of course, until quite recently the orthodox view was precisely that when the capitalist structure was going up in the flames of war, the Communist castle in Spain would be built!

In this situation our hope both for the abolition of war and for the achievement of a better social order rests in turning around the Leninist argument about the inseparable connection between war and an imperialist economy and setting it on its feet.

Let us grant the relationship here indicated, grant that so long as your economic order is based largely on greed and strife, involves a mad competitive race for markets and investment opportunities, etc., it is an idle dream that you can abolish war. Let us grant that if we genuinely want to abolish war, we shall not seek to maintain the imperialist set-up which dominates the world today and that there is ample justification for the scorn which revolutionists have heaped upon the so-called pacifism which is sentimental and naïve, which is wedded to the economic and political status quo, which is against war in general but always able to swallow the particular war which is on at the moment.

But if it is impossible effectively to hit war without striking at an exploiting imperialist economy, then if we did really strike at war, would that not mean striking imperialism at its very heart? Can we imagine how a modern system of exploitation can be kept going if it has no war-machine and if it cannot make war? Today it is unquestionably, it seems to me, the possession of a military machine, its maintenance, the possibility of resorting to war, which keep an exploiting capitalism and a predatory imperialism alive, which constantly interfere with the movement for social justice, and make it possible for ruling groups to evade facing and dealing with the economic evils which bring suffering upon the masses. And it is the masses who make this possible, who manufacture and transport the armaments of war, man the militias and the armies, and obediently wage the wars!

Let us pause to illustrate this crucial point with concrete evidence. The money for modern armament comes out of the social services. We have not been able to get an adequate housing program in the United States—the budget had to be balanced. The need to balance the budget suddenly disappeared when a billion and a quarter supernavy program had to be added to a half-billion dollar navy appropriation which already constituted the biggest peacetime appropriation in our history. Speedily even such "defense" expenditures were deemed inadequate.

The masses themselves constantly have their minds diverted from the economic injustice and the handicaps under which they suffer by war propaganda, war scares, the whipping up of nationalistic or racial prejudice against people of a potential enemy nation. When nothing else will do to avert dangerous revolt, this is a sure-fire remedy.

The armaments industry, so long as the war method is not renounced, is coddled, and thus a group with strong anti-labor and reactionary tendencies is built up. An armaments boom always provides an ideal escape from the dilemmas into which a profit economy falls. For, as Brailsford and others have pointed out, on the one hand, it requires large amounts of capital which are lying idle, and on the other hand, it does not throw new goods for purchase and consumption on the market which is already glutted because the masses lack the purchasing power to buy back what they have produced. Presently, the nation confronts the alternative of a depression because of the collapse of this armaments boom or an adventure into war with another nation which has been indulging in a similar boom and is threatened with a similar crash. In either case, the movement toward better social conditions for the masses suffers another set-back.

If at the moment war cannot be risked and the masses threaten to revolt against the miseries of another depression, then the armaments and the military personnel which they have themselves helped to build are used to suppress their struggle. For it is not against the people of another country that a nation's armaments are used in the first instance. That occurs only when war actually breaks out. A nation's armies and armaments are used in the first instance against its own people, against labor and every liberal, progressive, radical tendency in the nation—used psychologically as a constant threat or actually, physically, as in strikes and against anti-militarist and other popular demonstrations. Is it possible to find in history a single instance of a great army or military machine whose primary and often exclusive function over a period of years was not exploitation of the home population or of another backward or subject people, the exploitation of the former being in that case temporarily alleviated? Furthermore, as has recently again been pointed out in Vagt's most suggestive *History of Militarism*, within any régime, save for a very brief period at the high point of a revolution, the army is an instrument of the conservative or reactionary elements in that régime. "Revolutionary" armies, as in France in the eighteenth century, slay the revolution that brings them into being. The very essence of military organization and discipline, of the military mind, leads to this result.

By the same token nothing shakes the morale of reactionary interests so profoundly as the discovery that they cannot rely on the army. It is their confidence that in the end it will be possible to maintain their military machine and to dupe the masses into engaging in another war that constitutes the psychological basis of their power. Taking that away from them, by having the people make it clear that they can no longer be duped into maintaining armaments and making war, would do far more than terrorism and violence to unseat exploiters and to remove obstructions to the movement for social justice.

Just as such thorough-going war-resistance as we have been discussing would greatly facilitate the movement for a better social order within the nation, even so it is indispensable to the movement for appeasement and justice among the nations which is likewise an integral part of the movement toward a better social order. Suppose the British Labor party had adhered to its anti-militarist tradition and refused a few years ago to support the rearmament policy of the Tory government, what would it have signified? One thing above all, namely that Great Britain could not and would not by force of arms seek to maintain the present imperialist status quo. It would have indicated a readiness, even at some sacrifice, to refuse to participate in another armaments race, to alter the present inequalities in access to raw materials, to bring down tariff barriers. But this is the road out of the horrible international crisis in which the world finds itself.

One other, and most important, way in which militarism, war preparations, and war impede and indeed defeat the movement for social justice and progress must be cited. The moment you admit that war eventually has to be resorted to and that therefore war-preparations have to be made—since it is then obviously silly to be unprepared—you strengthen the hands of reactionaries, of the potential Fascist elements, even in the democratic nation. Psychologically this is the case, since those elements are in a position to say: "We told you so. You are now admitting that in the last analysis war is the only sure means to defend the things we value most. But you pacifists, labor people, liberals, dreamers, what not, have delayed adequate preparations so long that now in the interest of national self-respect, democracy, fidelity to our international obligations, and peace itself, we must enter upon a swift and huge rearmament program!"

Furthermore, the nation must then begin to make plans for war-mobilization and some steps toward carrying out such plans must be taken—steps toward regimentation and fascism and away from freedom and social improvement. When war comes, then with it comes fascism, since only by regimentation of the extremest sort can modern warfare be waged, and even if in some favorably situated nation a measure of democracy is restored, the movement for better conditions for the masses has again suffered an agonizing postponement, the gains made by labor through years of struggle are again wiped out.

Not then by the road of another general war or a series of wars but by the road of the abolition of war can we move to a sounder economy and a finer civilization.

At this point some of my acquaintances in the radical movement, who have come to recognize that something more is needed than the repetition of outworn clichés, are likely to comment on my proposal of a thorough-going pacifism or war-resistance as the sound strategy for achieving social progress: "It would be a good trick, if it would work, but you can't get the masses, you can't get labor to adopt the policy."

To which, it seems to me, the reply is that labor, the workers, are not born Marxist-Leninists either. It is only by a terrific amount of organizational and educational activity, accompanied by countless sacrifices, and marked by frequent set-backs, that a revolutionary group gains enough influence over the masses to accomplish—what? To gain the chance to lead these masses on a course that seems foredoomed to failure, that is to say, the chance in some desperate crisis when war has wrought vast destruction, to seize power and set up a dictatorship which ostensibly aims at democracy, plenty, and peace.

Surely, there is a chance—a chance which men who feel and can still reason must eagerly seize—that if we spent as much time, energy, devotion, sacrifice, in trying to persuade all progressive forces in the nation to adopt an uncompromising anti-militarism, rejection of all war, civil and international, we might succeed in winning mass-support for such a course. And this course, as we must now proceed to indicate, holds far greater promise of benefit for mankind if it measurably succeeds.

The method of complete refusal to support or tolerate a war-machine, accompanied, of course, by economic and political organization of labor and the other progressive elements in the community, is not open to the charge that this is "mere liberalism"—with the emphasis on "mere"— an utterly ineffective "gradualism," an attempt at solution by compromise which does not go down to the roots of things. To the contrary, such war-resistance has genuinely revolutionary implications. As we have already remarked, a little reflection will show that it is really not possible for an exploiting imperialist régime to keep going if it is deprived of its war-machine and of its ability to resort to war. On the other hand, ruling out the possibility of resort to war by any modern nation is bound to have tremendous repercussions in the cultural, political, and economic spheres of the nation's life. Surely no student of the modern labor and revolutionary movement would argue that in the history of that movement departure from an uncompromising anti-militarism (voting war-credits to a bourgeois government, for example) is ever an indication that the movement is becoming more revolutionary.

But it is true that a pacifist "revolution" would not involve the complete scrapping of all liberalism, of all democratic process, and all parliamentary machinery. Those who reject the way of violence will insist that it is precisely the movement for social change which has most to gain by using to the full such, admittedly as yet imperfect, democratic machinery as men have developed, and by making it clear that even under pressure and severe provocation it will not be jockeyed into dependence upon violence.

Unless the movement of social reform or radicalism comes to understand this, it will help to encompass its own defeat. There has been a tendency among radicals, in revolting against sham liberalism, to espouse illiberalism. It is not clear that in this, any more than in any other sphere, it is wise and efficient to throw out the baby with the bath. Similarly, to argue, as has in effect often been done, that democracy has only been imperfectly realized, much so-called democracy is camouflaged dictatorship of a class, therefore we must get rid of democracy and embrace some kind of dictatorship, some choice as to the color of shirt to be worn being allowed—this is neither good logic nor good politics.

A pacifist "revolution" could succeed only if the consent of a decisive majority of the population were obtained. This is equivalent to saying that only by the development of a high degree of unity, solidarity, faith, morale, passion, among the workers and all who desire a better world, could thorough-going social changes by non-violent methods be achieved. That would imply that these elements would not have evaded those problems of working-class unity, of sound and effective strategy and tactics in accomplishing social change, which as a matter of fact are constantly being evaded by them, because in the back of their minds lurks the idea that violence will cut the really difficult Gordian knots at the critical moment.

Violence is often an "escape" for the radical and the revolutionist, just as it is for the reactionary and counter-revolutionist. The latter does not honestly face himself and the problems of the society in which he lives, because he believes that when things go too far he can put the troublesome Reds in jail or call out the troops to shoot them down or persuade the would-be Reds themselves that their real enemies are the people of another country and that a war must be launched against them. In much the same way social radicals evade puzzling issues by telling themselves in so many words: "One of these days we'll settle these matters by turning the guns on the capitalists; and under the dictatorship we shall then institute, we shall also take the bothersome fellows in our own movement who do not agree with us, and stand them up against the wall and shoot them."

Let us illustrate our point from current situations which are of the greatest significance for this argument. In 1920, through the so-called Kapp Putsch, an attempt was made to establish a reactionary military dictatorship in Germany. Kapp marched his troops into Berlin and "took over the government." The duly constituted government moved out. In about a week Kapp marched his forces out again and abandoned the attempt to set up a dictatorship. What had happened? The great German labor movement and other progressive elements had carried out a policy of "non-co-operation" with Kapp. They had inaugurated a general strike. As someone has put it, Kapp "pushed the buttons" in his office and expected the telephone and telegraph to respond, the lights to work, the gasoline for his troops to be available, the trains to bring food for them—but none of these things happened. The skilled men had disconnected the delicate and intricate mechanisms of a modern industrial economy at crucial points, the masses failed to give that active and passive support to a usurping régime on which so much depends. Kapp was defeated.

To the pacifist who argues that similar methods might have stopped Hitler, the reply will be made that Hitler's forces and Hitler's program were much better organized than Kapp's. And this will be correct. But it is also true that between Kapp and the accession of Hitler to power many things happened to the labor and progressive movement in Germany of which account must be taken if we are to understand how fascism comes to power and how its advance might be stopped. I refer, for example, to the divisions within the German labor movement itself which caused Communists at one stage actually to co-operate with the Nazis in strikes in Berlin in order to embarrass the Social-Democratic administration in Prussia; to the fact that many leaders and members of the Social-Democratic trade unions had become thoroughly middle-class and capitalistic in their psychology and toward the last were not so much concerned with combating Hitlerism as with coming to some understanding with it. The significant fact about the labor and revolutionary movement in "the classic land of Marxism" was that when Hitler came to power, it did not make a gesture either of violent or of non-violent resistance. Surely something tragic and horrible must have happened to the morale of a movement to bring it to such a pass of impotence in a crisis. The fact is that before Hitler came to power, great multitudes of German workers, utterly disheartened by the confusion of counsels, the factional bitterness, and other developments in their own movement, had lost all faith in its effectiveness and saving power, even though in many cases they were not conscious of what had taken place in their own souls and to the last displayed a touching loyalty to the movement and the philosophy which they had expected would bring a new world into being. It has not yet been demonstrated that a radical or popular movement which retains its morale, its faith in itself, can be overcome with mere brute force, by violence. "The Egyptians are men and not gods; and their horses are flesh and not spirit"—and it is only when there is no longer "spirit," when there is but "flesh," force, violence, to oppose them that they are able to conquer.

Observations looking in a similar direction may be made about Spain, another situation upon which, it is commonly held, pacifists can shed no light. For many years Spanish régimes have alternated between what may for convenience and in order to beg as few questions as possible, be described as progressive and conservative ones. Whenever a conservative government took office, frequently after a coup d'état, it had the task of "making good" in office. In practice that meant relieving the lot of the peasants and workers. This a régime bent upon defending special interests was unable to accomplish. Thus such régimes were repeatedly overthrown—not altogether, yet in the main, by non-violent means: strikes, agitation, non-payment of taxes, demand for elections, and so on. A progressive or popular government would win out in the election, take office, and as likely as not be forced out again by a "putsch." Then the pattern described would be repeated again. The last time a popular government was overthrown tens of thousands were put into jail. That did not kill the progressive movement. In 1936 it took office again—the recent Loyalist government.

At that time important measures were neglected. The army, which like every army was essentially a bulwark of reaction, was retained. There was only a small measure of reorganization. Had a serious effort been made, amid the first popular enthusiasm over the accession of the new government, at dismantling this reactionary institution—and there was a real possibility of doing something then—the reactionaries would have been deprived of a powerful instrument. To cite another instance, because of divided counsels the Loyalist government took no steps to deal with the land question in a radical way. This is one of the reasons why the Franco régime had as much peasant support as it had. The understandable but nevertheless unsound and fanatical hatred of all religion and all religious persons on the part of many left wingers tended toward the same result. Most important of all is, in my opinion, the fact that the Loyalist government kept the Spanish (imperialist) Army in Morocco. Had it taken courageous steps to put an end to Spanish domination over the Moors, is it reasonable to suppose that it would have been possible to induce the Moors to make war upon their liberators?

Even if all these considerations bearing upon the strategy and tactics of social change are put to one side for the moment, it is at least debatable whether today the Spanish people and the popular movement in Spain would be any worse off than they are now if when Franco undertook his putsch the Loyalist government had said to Franco in effect: "You have no right to overthrow this government. If you do, we shall not co-operate with you. We shall keep up the struggle against your régime as we have against its predecessors. Again we shall challenge you to do something about the case of Spanish peasants and workers. But we will not let you jockey us into a situation where we against our wills help to involve Spain in civil war; we will not answer violence with violence." Doubtless there would have been deeds of tyranny and terrorism. But it seems reasonable to think more Spanish people would be alive today, less of Spain's resources would be laid waste, it would have been more difficult for Hitler and Mussolini and Chamberlain and their like to make Spain the victim in a cruel game of imperialist jockeying for position in the next world war. Such resistance by essentially non-violent means plus the ineptitude of reactionary governments has often enough in similar cases availed to undermine the latter.

Salvador de Madariaga, former Spanish Ambassador to the United States, in a recent important broadcast to this country has made the significant statement: "As a Spaniard, I want to say in all sincerity, and having reflected on this subject during two harrowing years, that if in the Spring of 1936 the working class of Spain, led by well meaning but inexperienced leaders, had not rushed into a meaningless revolution, the military revolt would have had no chances whatsoever."

The point of our present argument is, however, that these considerations to which we have pointed regarding the failure of the radical movement to develop its own unity and morale, etc. cannot honestly and safely be left out of account by its members and friends. If the movement neglects these essentials, then repeatedly tries to shift the blame from its own shoulders by asserting that fascism comes to power by brute force, purely because the Fascists have more guns and castor oil, and can be prevented or overcome only by brute force, the movement for social change will encounter disaster in one country after another. It must adopt that basic attitude inculcated by the prophets and Jesus of taking out first the beam from its own eye; it must recognize that defeat comes to the movement for social justice and democracy primarily from within as it fails by self-discipline to achieve solidarity and fraternity in its own ranks. Fascism is a force that, as it were, rushes into the social vacuum thus created; the battle has been lost before the bludgeons and the castor oil are brought into play. If the progressive forces everywhere fail to learn this lesson, then on a large scale they will be playing into the hands of their enemies, as strikers not infrequently play into the hands of certain reactionary and hard-boiled employers, when they fall into the use of violence which these employers have found it profitable to provoke by spending tens of thousands of dollars for labor spies and strong arm squads.

One more observation must be made at this point. As has just now been suggested, to a great degree the violence used by the masses is deliberately provoked by reactionary vested interests, and even where this is not the case, it results from the wearing out of the patience of oppressed people, their despair of obtaining by peaceful means redress of the most elementary grievances. Practically no one would question today that this was the case in the revolt of the Russian people in 1917. The Tsarist régime had sowed the wind and reaped the whirlwind. I speak from personal observation and experience when I testify that for the most part strikes are won not by violence but by what amounts in the main to non-violent resistance— by the amazing solidarity, courage, patience, and self-sacrifice of the workers. Most capable labor leaders strive sincerely to keep a strike from becoming a matching of force with force, if only because they recognize that the forces of reaction always have the preponderance in weapons. It is, in other words, on essentially spiritual weapons that they depend, not least on the capacity of the workers to stand shoulder to shoulder and to sacrifice for a common cause—a point obviously of great significance for our whole argument. When, however, full allowance has been made for these facts, it must be added that those who argue that the futility of the way of non-violence has been conclusively proved in the history of labor and the movement for a new social order in the modern world, and that consequently there is no way out save that of violence, are guilty of over-simplifying the situation. The fact is that the way of non-violence has not been given a real test. For it is over-simplification to read the struggle as one between embittered and violent capitalists, reactionaries, and Fascists—devils, in other words—and pure, angelic workers, farmers, trade unionists, Socialists, anarchists, Communists who proceed always in the spirit and by the method of non-violence. The motives of "have-nots" are, alas, often much like those of "haves." Many on both sides espouse the doctrine that the end (their end of course) justifies the means. An influential minority has always preached the doctrine that no class in power will give up its position and plunder voluntarily, and therefore the transfer of power necessarily involves civil war. The movement for social change will have to make a radical decision for or against violence. For if you hold that at the critical moment it is upon the arbitration of the sword that you must depend, then, as we have already pointed out, you must seek to be as well prepared and armed as possible, you will hold it to be a solemn duty to accustom the masses to the belief that they must be ready to use violence, you will act upon the assumption that the offense may at times be the best defense—in short, violence then inevitably becomes a major factor in the situation, means are bound to be employed which, in civil as in international war, are impossible to control and which thwart and corrupt the end one seeks. This brings us to a second part of the elucidation of the way of non-violence in social change.

Chapter VI

Pacifism as Revolutionary
Strategy—II

WE HAVE TRIED TO SHOW THAT THE PRACTICE OF A THOROUGH-
GOING RENUNCIATION OF WAR, MAKING IT IMPOSSIBLE FOR A
nation to wage war, would indeed be "revolutionary" in
its effects in all spheres of economic and political life,
though it would not mean the renunciation of democratic
process and true liberalism, but rather the honest practice
of them. We have indicated also that the labor and radical
movements have not practiced a philosophy and strategy
of genuine and consistent non-violence, that frequently
rather they have neglected important and elementary internal problems, such as factionalism, and having been
weakened as a result of such neglect have then come to
feel that there is no way of overcoming reaction save
brute force.

We must now elaborate upon a suggestion made earlier
in this essay and point out that if we seek under modern
conditions to achieve a new social order by the road of
violence, our efforts are doomed to defeat in advance. To
achieve "the revolution" by this method means that the
new order starts off with a dictatorship dependent in its

turn upon such instruments as an army, a Gaypayoo, revolutionary tribunals, and the like. These generate poisons which destroy the régime which depends upon them. We must of necessity turn again to the examples presented in the history of the bolshevik régime in Russia. Pointing out how partially sound economic ideas and a great idealism have been thwarted there, and prevented from accomplishing more than a small part of what had been hoped for, does not make us enemies of those ideas or despisers of that idealism.

Consider how the instrument of revolutionary dictatorship has evolved. In the system of Marx-Lenin the proletariat, considered in the abstract, is the class destined by history to usher in a scientific and class-less civilization. It is the new Messiah, the bringer of true and complete democracy. The actual proletarians, however, the bricklayers, railroad men, miners, factory hands, are not as a rule aware of the mission entrusted to their class. They cannot be trusted to achieve the revolution. There must therefore be a party composed of the elite, the most conscious and intelligent elements of the working-class and the intellectuals. It must manipulate the proletariat into accomplishing its historic mission. The party comes to be thought and spoken of in exalted, mystical terms. It has the deposit of the truth; in effect, it can, like the king, "do no wrong." Because of this, and because the danger of counter-revolution must be guarded against, it is held that there shall be only one party, the party of the revolution. If there were two parties, one would be right, the other wrong and hence counter-revolutionary, and why clutter up the scene with a wrong party? (It is hardly necessary to note that in these matters dictatorships of the Right and of the Left follow essentially the same pattern.) Clearly under such conditions the party exercises a virtual dictatorship over the masses. Genuine political life and activity can go on only in the party. In Russia it is obvious that the Soviets, popular organs of democracy, rapidly deteriorated in significance in comparison with the party and its organs.

Within the party itself the completest democracy must obtain—in theory. The aim of "the revolution" is the achievement of genuine democracy as against the spurious bourgeois brand that exists in capitalist nations. Bolshevik theory recognizes that the instrument upon which above all dependence is placed for ending exploitation and tyranny must itself be democratic. But the practice turns out to be quite different. Even in the periods when party life was most vigorous and least bureaucratized and when it was headed by a great human being such as Lenin, whose intellect and self-confidence were such that he never needed to fear discussion, it was expected that once a decision had been arrived at, presumably by a thoroughly democratic discussion, the individual should sacrifice his conscience, if need be, to the party, that there should be iron discipline in carrying out decisions. All possibility of organized, effective criticism from without has been removed by the outlawing of all rival political organs. Under such circumstances, the inevitable trend to bureaucratism gets under way and the bureaucracy is armed with a Gaypayoo. The party becomes "totalitarian," absolutist, in character, and its members pawns in its hands, the more so because members are required to renounce all idealistic systems of philosophy and to accept the metaphysics of dialectical materialism—the party, that is to say, is not a mere political party in the ordinary sense, exercising a certain amount of control or influence over some spheres of the individual's life; it is a combination of a political party and a religious order wielding the state machinery of a dictatorship.

Thus the party in effect exercises a dictatorship over its own members as well as over the masses. But the process does not stop there. Presently there can be no genuine discussion within the party itself. If there were an honest conflict over an important political issue, this would inevitably become known among the masses. They would be drawn into the discussion. But this would mean in effect that there were two parties, and this cannot be permitted for reasons already stated. Consequently, we get a dictatorship of the executive, known as the Political Bureau in the Bolshevik party, over the party.

The process does not end there. Presently it becomes impossible to have a genuine discussion in the Political Bureau. There are too many "secrets" which it might be dangerous to communicate to the general membership. If there were a genuine discussion in the Bureau, that would inevitably get out among the membership, and so among the masses. That would again mean giving up the one monolithic party system. Thus the dictatorship of the Political Bureau over the party eventuates in the dictatorship of the Executive Secretary over the former. The one-man dictator must then proceed to stamp out all potential rivals. Above all this will mean the men who rose to power with him. They are also strong men, the halo of "the revolution" still crowns them, worst of all they know the unsavory secrets of the "practical measures" that were "necessary" in order to achieve the dictatorship first of the ruling group, then of the "strong man" over that group. It is not necessary to dwell upon the tragedy this involves for the aims of the revolution, for those, to use André Gide's phrase, "who made the revolution as distinct from those who profit by it." If one is interested in a sad and moving account of certain phases of that tragedy there is Gide's *Return to the U.S.S.R.*

We must remind ourselves of a second point touched upon earlier in this essay. A revolution which begins by building a great "Red Army" creates an instrumentality which from the very character of its organization and discipline will, except perhaps for a very brief period, be an agency to beget conformism and to protect social conservatism rather than to produce independence and encourage social change. There is that about an army—and history does not indicate that "revolutionary" armies (contradiction in terms?) are an exception—which causes its commanders to speak or at any rate to act like one of Napoleon's marshals, Lefebvre, who, thundering the slogans of the French Revolution, said to the burgomasters of "liberated," i.e., conquered, Franconia: "We have come to bring you liberty and equality—but don't let that go to your heads, for the first one of you who moves without my permission will be shot."

Observe, also, how the "dialectic" of violence works out. Lenin repeatedly warned the inner circle of the Russian Bolshevik party not to make the mistake of the leaders of the French Revolution and begin to kill each other off. In effect the Bolshevik teaching about terrorism meant therefore: "You will have to kill off some landlords and capitalists who will not voluntarily relinquish their power and privilege. You may have to shoot—liquidate—some of the richer peasants, even some workers who don't understand that the revolution is their revolution and carried out for their good. Not, of course, because you enjoy doing these things, but because it is the only realistic way for a practical man to proceed in the world as it is now constituted." (Have no doubt that Bolsheviks are as honest and idealistic about these matters as good Christian people when they go to war, reluctantly and as the only "realistic" thing to do.) "But keep the violence under control. Use terrorism, but don't let it become your master. Don't make the mistake of the leaders of the French Revolution and begin killing each other off in the inner circle of the party." But that is exactly what they have come to!

In other words, achieve or seek to protect your revolution by violence, build your machine for terrorism, repression, your revolutionary tribunals, your pervasive system of espionage with what that means for those who practice it and those upon whom it is practiced, elevate ruthlessness into a major virtue—for the time being, you tell yourself, of course, as men always do when they take up the sword—and presently this machine, like every machine, tends to perpetuate itself, you have to resort to repeated doses of repression and terrorism, and the means you use thwart and corrupt your end, so that the result is far from that fair goal of which you dreamed.

We have now sought to show that the way of dictatorship and violence has been found wanting as an instrument for achieving a new order, and that the way of thorough-going pacifism which has not been given a genuine trial would prove "revolutionary" in its effects on the social and political order. We may here point to two considerations which may be said to be of a "tactical" character, in favor of adopting the method of non-violence.

In the first place, it is now generally recognized that the balance of power in deciding whether a people shall turn toward reaction or toward social progress rests with certain sections of the middle class—farmers, the better paid workers, technicians, small business people, professional people. The history of the post-war period has, I think, made quite clear that the hope of winning a decisive percentage of these people in industrialized countries to join with the industrial workers in a violent revolution is doomed to disappointment. If the workers and left wing intellectuals renounce the democratic process, for whatever reason, and make it known that they depend upon the sword to say the last word, the reactionaries and Fascists are given the opportunity which they covet to pose as the defenders of order and national integrity. Even if at last no believers in peaceful and democratic process remain to claim the allegiance of the masses, multitudes of these middle class elements will choose a Fascist rather than a Communist dictatorship —Hague of Jersey City and a red, white, and blue shirt, rather than Earl Browder and a red shirt. The hope of the progressive movement lies in making it clear that at any cost and no matter what the provocation, it will adhere to democratic ways and will refuse to take the sword. In this as in the international field, Robert Hillyer's warning holds good: "If peace has lost her war, there is no other thing worth fighting for."

Closely connected with this point is another, namely, that the movement for a new social order based upon the ideals of the Jewish-Christian prophetic tradition is much more likely to win the support of the churches, which have been born of this tradition, if this movement clings to the way of democracy and non-violence. There are in these churches two groups which must be considered in this connection. On the one hand are the more conservative elements. What a movement for social change dominated by the philosophy and strategy of orthodox Marxism-Leninism says in effect to these elements is: "If we win, then we shall liquidate you, destroy your churches, stamp out religion of all sorts." (We need not pause to argue here that as a matter of fact a very fanatical form of false religion will be organized into a state-church.) Surely a revolutionary movement which takes such a position must be capable either of great stupidity or of great duplicity if it pretends to expect anything but hostility from these elements in the Jewish and Christian churches which it openly threatens with liquidation. If there be no other alternative, these more conservative elements will inevitably seek to come to some sort of interim understanding with Fascism rather than signing their own death-warrant without any hope of reprieve. What would become of a Niemöller in the Soviet Union today?

The more progressive elements in the churches, on the other hand, will in the main combine their social radicalism with pacifism or non-violence. The exceptions are and will be fairly numerous, but they will be exceptions. In the Jewish-Christian prophetic tradition, as we have pointed out in previous chapters, profound inner religious experience and social passion are combined in a distinctive and often disturbing fashion. That God appears to Moses in the Burning Bush means that Moses must form a union of exploited brickmakers and lead them out of bondage. At the beginning of the Law stand significantly the words: "*I* am the Lord thy God which have brought thee out of the land of Egypt, out of the house of slavery." For Jesus to be "the Son of God" means that he must "proclaim liberty to the captives and preach good news to the poor."

But as the names of Isaiah and Jeremiah and Jesus and the early Christians and St. Francis and John Woolman remind us, and as has been brilliantly and exhaustively set forth in such books as Franz Werfel's great novel about Jeremiah, *Hearken Unto The Voice*, John Cournos' *Open Letter to Jews and Christians*, G. D. H. MacGregor's *New Testament Basis of Pacifism*, Charles Rann Kennedy's *The Terrible Meek*, and many other works ancient and modern, the method of social redemption adopted by the men who have this combination of profound inner spiritual experience and social passion, which is characteristic of the Jewish-Christian prophetic outlook, is the method of the "Suffering Servant of Jehovah," the way of the Cross not of the Sword, the way of those who have entered into "that spirit which taketh away the occasion of all wars," of those who know that the devil cannot be depended upon to cast out the devil, of those who really believe in the overcoming power of prayer and humility and sacrifice. The way of violence has always seemed to them to be essentially "Satanic," and necessarily so since it violates the conception of God as not Might or Law or Wisdom or even primarily Virtue, but as Righteousness, Social Righteousness, Father, Love, Fellowship. They cannot conceive of God as a heavenly potentate and general, hence God's Messiah for them can never use the method of the earthly potentate and general—least of all in the cause of good, of the Kingdom, which cannot possibly come by evil means.

If, therefore, the most earnest and socially conscious and profoundly religious spirits in the church are told: "In order to be a good socialist, you must be a revolutionary militarist," the result can only be to divide and to sap the morale of potential battlers for social change. For from such a demand these spirits will sadly yet firmly turn away, and if necessary play again the rôle of the Remnant which holds to the ways of the spirit and seems utterly ineffective over against the "realists" of the Right and the Left, but outlasts Pharaoh and Nebuchadnezzar and Cæsar and Barabbas and Hitler and Mussolini and Stalin.

What has already been said about the effectiveness of pacifism for accomplishing important changes in the economic order also implies that the danger of effective "counter-revolution" against such changes will be decidedly less than if an attempt is made to bring about a new order by the method of dictatorship and violence. The elements who will desire to undo the results achieved will be much fewer and probably less insistent and vigorous about returning to the past. Reactionaries will not be able to argue that the changes have been accomplished by a putsch engineered by a minority. They will not have personal grievances based upon the cruelties inflicted upon their relatives and friends, such cruelties being invariably a part of a violent revolution.

In the course of a "pacifist revolution" a vast amount of

educational work will have been done, and the attitudes of men will have been changed. For it is manifestly an essential part of the non-violent approach to life not to trust merely to changing the environment, forcibly, or at any rate from outside, altering economic and political mechanisms, and to expect that this will give us a better world. The pacifist will lay stress upon the enlightenment of minds and re-direction of wills. Thus change will have been prepared for. Public opinion in its favor will be so strong and so firmly based that it will seem futile to oppose it.

Another factor which will work in the same direction is the unity and solidarity which will prevail among the workers, who will not have evaded the issue raised by factionalism and corruption in their own ranks, and then rationalized their resort to violence as inevitable and as forced upon them entirely by others from without. There will also be, as previously indicated, fewer people from the middle class desiring a return to the past.

If a revolution is achieved by violence, there are certain to be many people—presently even, as Russia shows, among the supporters of the revolutionary régime itself—whose friends and relatives have suffered at the hands of the secret police. Such people are bound to be actual or potential threats to the stability of the régime. A non-violent revo-lution will not face this problem.

A revolution of the latter type will involve much less disorganization of economic and political life. The insecu-rity and suffering resulting from this disorganization con-stitute a perplexing and often tragic problem even for the most honest and efficient revolutionary régime. They may furnish a basis for counter-revolutionary activity. It may appear to take somewhat longer to achieve drastic economic reforms by non-violent and democratic means, but when account is taken of the long and difficult transition required after a violent revolution to overcome the effects of the destruction of resources and the dislocation of economic mechanisms, the former method turns out to be more sure and rapid. Indeed there is good reason to doubt whether the outcome of revolution by civil war in a highly industrialized country could possibly be economic progress, and would not rather involve retrogression for a considerable period at least to a lower type of economy.

One more aspect of the problem of a post-revolutionary régime must be touched upon. The policy of repression and terrorism into which such a régime is apparently bound to fall produces the resentment to which we have already referred. But, paradoxical as it may seem, it produces also conformism. Men accept regimentation. They get into the habit of waiting for the party manifesto to tell them what to think. Liberals and radicals do not fail to point out this feature of Fascist dictatorships. André Gide, Eugene Lyons, and others have pointed to a similar development in Russia. But, obviously, to a socialist and democratic revolution such conformism and deadening of the mind and spirit are more dangerous than avowed counter-revolution. By such means the very springs of democratic and brotherly life are poisoned.

The question has sometimes been put to advocates of non-violence whether pacifist leaders could "handle" a revolutionary situation suddenly precipitated, for example, by defeat in war. The pacifist, as we have pointed out, will not seek such a situation. His philosophy puts him on guard against short cuts. He will even seek to avoid propagandizing or tricking people by high pressure emotionalism into accepting the pacifist philosophy—or more accurately, professing to accept it. He is bound to respect the personality of his fellowman. He desires assent from within, not outer conformity.

Obviously, too, a pacifist movement which was ill-disciplined, had not thought through its problems, and lacked competent technicians would be exactly as helpless in such a crisis of social disintegration as we are envisaging as a non-pacifist party would be. But assume that provision were made to meet the requirements just mentioned, as Gandhi's Satyagraha movement in India is consciously attempting to do. (See a most illuminating discussion of the matter in K. Shridharani's *War Without Violence*.) Then there appears to me to be no a priori reason why a movement based on non-violence could not undertake the re-organization of community life in its various phases even more competently than a non-pacifist organization. As a matter of fact, an essential feature of a revolution which follows defeat in war, as did the Russian, is a revulsion on the part of the masses against war. The soldiers lay down their arms. They turn back in masses to their homes and to the ancient peaceful pursuits of the human race. Furthermore, in its early stages the transfer of power is likely to be almost bloodless. The old order simply collapses. The new régime does not so much seize power in a climactic struggle as pick up power which has fallen from the nerveless hands of former rulers.

Left wing historians have themselves frequently pointed to such phenomena. The stock Leninist explanation of the violence which later breaks out is that the remnants of the old régime, when they have recovered from their first fright, sabotage the efforts of the revolutionary government to rebuild industry, and engage in positive, violent counter-revolutionary activity against which the new régime must defend itself. Unquestionably this is true of some representatives of the old order. But this is by no means the whole story. In no small measure the bitterness and strife that marked the early months and years of the Russian Revolution sprang from the systematic persecution by the Bolsheviks of all who would not bow slavishly to the party line. Even in those early days the party's high-handedness and brutality drove many of the most idealistic elements into the opposition. Violence against landlords and even against kulaks, the somewhat more well-to-do-peasants, was condoned and often deliberately encouraged. Fear led to terroristic practices, and then fear that such practices would be avenged led to more terrorism. It was not many years after the Revolution that Lenin and Trotzky actually used the Red Army against the sailors of Kronstadt who had played a superbly heroic rôle in the most critical hours of the Revolution! Naturally the violence which was in part, at least, provoked by such attitudes and actions on the part of the Bolsheviks was regarded as justifying further repression and violence. The vicious circle to which the pacifist has so often pointed was again complete. Then the fighting retarded recovery and indeed served to carry further the process of economic disorganization which the war had begun. Thus more dissatisfaction, bitterness, fear, starvation developed, appearing to call for more machinery of repression.

A non-violent organization in such a situation would be in a position to take full advantage of the revulsion against war being experienced by the masses and of their desire to get back to their homes and normal occupations. It would make full use of the energies a people feel under such circumstances arising from the sense of liberation from the ancient yoke, the feeling of having entered the promised land. There is also at such moments a joyous sense of brotherhood among the masses, which causes them to embrace each other, to join in jubilant songs, to share their goods, to endure gladly the greatest sacrifices. Why should we expect that men who have embraced a purely materialistic philosophy of life, who do not believe that there are objective moral standards, who have no genuine respect for the individual but only for "the mass," who believe in dictatorship—why should we expect such men, for all the admirable qualities some of them may have, to be able to help the masses to build a fair and stable order? On the other hand, what might not men who had qualities of leadership, who were technically competent, and who had the spirit of Jesus, who were prepared to build on the idealism, the abhorrence of war, the will to peace, the sense of fraternity, the capacity for sacrifice which characterize the masses in such creative moments of history— what might they not achieve? Certainly it must be granted that in view of the actual course of events in Russia, it is debatable whether such a pacifist leadership would not be more practically successful.

As for the query about whether foreign invaders would not overthrow the new régime, we may point out that when an army lays down its arms, a country is in any case open to invasion. Lenin had to make the "peace" of Brest-Litovsk with the Germans. But when I note the reluctance with which men today go to war even when obviously hostile armies and navies are arrayed against them and they naturally believe that if they do not kill they will be killed, I find no good reason for supposing that any army could be gotten to invade a people which flatly renounced war. To the contrary, were any nation today to accept avowedly pacifist leadership, disband its army, offer to join with all others in really establishing a new order, the effect would be revolutionary. The Russian Revolution, it will be recalled, profoundly moved the masses of men, and for years caused economic and political over-lords throughout Europe to have uneasy dreams. But all that was nothing to the repercussions that would follow the spectacle of a nation led not by the Red Internationale but by the Internationale of Jesus whose banner is the Cross; a revolution not to establish the power of a new class equipped in turn with all the ancient paraphernalia of dictatorship, Chekas, secret police, armies, but to establish fraternity and therefore armed only with good-will and with trust in the equal desire of all peoples to escape from thralldom to war and tyranny. So far from a people which dared to take such a step being placed in jeopardy, they would be infinitely more safe than the Russians after 1917, for it must not be forgotten in this connection that refusal by British and French and other workers to transport munitions and troops for use against the Soviets did protect them in their early precarious years against attack by western imperialism.

Unless indeed European peoples are reduced by another

large-scale war to complete despair which would be the prelude to a return to the Dark Ages, the only leaders and movements they will trust in the new post-war period will be those who have resolutely opposed the war, and who renounce organized violence whether in civil or international life. Even after the last war the people in most countries which had really borne the brunt of the war, as we in the United States, of course, had not, turned upon those whom they regarded as responsible for the war, and put their faith in Communist, Socialist, and laborite leaders who had been opponents of war and who pledged themselves to policies guaranteed to end war. In the main, however, the latter believed that in class conflict violence was in greater or less degree necessary and efficacious and therefore justifiable. As we have already demonstrated, the way of violence and dictatorship has now been proved useless and destructive in this realm also. It is coming to be understood that techniques other than violence must be found by the movement for social justice, or it is doomed to utter annihilation. So eminent a personage as Hermann Rauschning has declared: "The day of fighting on the barricades has certainly passed. But the time in which passive resistance will become the revolutionary weapon of whole peoples seems, therefore, to have come and this weapon will be the more effective the more the whole economic apparatus becomes artificial and mechanized, the more massive and the more collectivized the whole mechanism of economic life." Unless, as we have said, the peoples lose hope entirely, the only leadership which will inspire any confidence after the war will be that which has stood out against the war and believes in the philosophy and strategy of non-violence. If the peoples as a whole no longer possess the energy to maintain an advanced economy, then in the midst of anarchy, the small groups who are committed to non-violence will constitute the nucleus through which eventually a new start may be made, much as did the little bands of Christians in the early centuries of our era.

Views such as those expressed in this essay would until quite recently have received scant consideration from workers and intellectuals who have been under the influence of the Marxist-Leninist philosophy. The post-war history of the revolutionary movement has, however, not been one of unqualified victory and uninterrupted progress. Today there is much talk of "the crisis of the Left." More than two years ago John Dos Passos wrote: "Of the hopes that dazzled the last twenty years that some political movement might tend to the betterment of the human lot little remains above ground but the tattered slogans of the past. These old slogans have enough magic in them to make them useful to gang leaders with a knack for organizing and a will to power, but their appeal is now of a pie-in-the-sky order and tends to be enforced with the bayonet, or in the case of a friend with the butt-end of a rifle."

As this quotation already suggests, the conviction is being expressed by a growing number of important writers of the Left that in large measure the crisis in the movement is due to its neglect of ethical factors, that the means men use determine the end they achieve, and that men who themselves lack honesty and integrity and gentleness cannot build a world of righteousness and brotherhood.

Thus Aldous Huxley, until recently one of the most sophisticated, cynical, and irreligious of novelists, has become passionately concerned about moral and religious problems and proclaims: "It is in the power of every individual to choose whether he shall deny or affirm the unity of mankind in an ultimate spiritual reality." And Professor Sidney Hook, the foremost student of Marx in the United States, reviewing Huxley's book, *Ends and Means*, roundly asserts: "With unerring insight Aldous Huxley has addressed himself to the basic moral problem of our times. His latest work is the moral credo of a passionate and distinguished intelligence. It is written primarily for professionally miscalled 'intellectuals' who have taken positions on how society is to be saved but who lack the wit or sensibility to test their positions by the means used to advance them. . . . Against those who would further the ultimate truth with immediate lies, counterpose to the uncritical worship of a leader an even more uncritical worship of a bigger leader, combat fascism with the methods of fascism—all on the ground that the end justifies the means—Huxley replies: 'The end cannot justify the means for the simple and obvious reason that the means employed determine the nature of the end produced.' The true Utopian is not he who criticizes society by the light of his ideals, even if he goes down to defeat; it is the self-styled realist who imagines he can realize his ideals by using methods which are bound to achieve their precise opposite."

One of the foremost theoreticians of the old Austrian Social-Democratic party, Willi Schlamm, has written a book with the significant title, *The Dictatorship of the Lie*, of which our distinguished American critic Edmund Wilson says: "His book is not a political program, nor is it properly even a manifesto. It is rather in the nature of a sermon. But it may be that what socialism needs at the moment is a few sermons like this of Schlamm. Certainly *The Dictatorship of the Lie* is one of the most bracing and air-clearing documents which have yet come out of the crisis of the Left."

Paraphrasing Schlamm, Wilson continues: "What is really behind all this [referring to the failure and in a sense the collapse of the secular revolutionary movement] is the elimination of moral principles from socialism. What are the claims to moral authority of an advance guard of social regeneration which has shown itself to be devoid of the primary human virtues of kindliness, fair-dealing, and veracity? There is no morality in the 'Dialectic.' . . . Nor does our social science of Marxism take us far. In that field our scientific knowledge is in reality still very meager, and the little we have succeeded in acquiring can never do duty for human initiative and human character. We must recognize that society has to be saved, not by the processes of a mystic dialectic, but by the influence of human beings who are self-respecting and morally sound."

Eugene Lyons in his recent best-seller, *Assignment In Utopia*, with great moral fervor contends that "the common denominator in all dictatorships is the decadence of the moral sense in mankind, the attrition of ethical values." He has become convinced that "the immediate task, for those who have the urge to participate consciously in the historic processes of their life time"—up to a few months ago that phrase would have been followed inevitably with some remark about achieving the political and economic revolution by any means at hand, but now the task "is to defend the basic concepts of freedom, humaneness, intellectual integrity, respect for life." This was written long before the Hitler-Stalin pact. It has, of course, served to open the eyes of many to the truth which Lyons and others have been proclaiming often in the face of bitter opposition.

W. H. Auden, perhaps the best loved of England's young revolutionary poets, sounds the same note in two passages in his most recent volume of poems, *On This Island:*

And out of the turf the bones of war continue;
"Know, then, cousin, the major cause of our collapse
Was a distortion in the human plastic by luxury produced.

Never higher than in our time were the vital advantages;
To matter entire, to the unbounded vigours of the instru-
          ment,
To all logical precision we were the rejoicing heirs.

But pompous, we assumed their power to be our own,
Believed machines to be our hearts' spontaneous fruit,
Taking our premises as shoppers take a tram.

While the disciplined love which alone could have em-
          ployed these engines
Seemed far too difficult and dull, and when hatred promised
An immediate dividend, all of us hated."

.   .   .   .   .

"Wind shakes the tree; the mountains darken;
And the heart repeats though we would not hearken:
'Yours is the choice, to whom the gods awarded
The language of learning and the language of love,
Crooked to move as a moneybug or a cancer
    Or straight as a dove.' "[1]

To cite but one more example out of dozens that are
readily available, Ignazio Silone is the foremost Italian
novelist of today. It is perhaps superfluous to remark that,
being an anti-Fascist, he does not reside in Italy. He
attained fame a few years ago with a novel entitled *Fonta-
mara* which means "bitter stream." It pictured village life
under fascism. A year or two ago he published *Bread And
Wine*, which is his portrayal of how fascism may be overcome. The hero of the book was in the secular revolutionary movement in Italy before Mussolini came to power.
Now, according to the story, he is back in Italy working
in the underground movement for a free régime, but with
a very different approach and methods from those previously employed. Here are some typical utterances which
Silone puts in the mouth of his hero:

The dictator's henchmen must be opposed not with
other henchmen who merely spoke differently, but with
men who lived and acted differently. . . . The evil I see
around me is deeper than politics. It is a canker. . . . There
is the class-struggle, the struggle between the town and
the country but underlying all these things there is man, a
poor, weak, terrified animal. The canker has penetrated
to his marrow. . . . All that remained alive and inde-
structible of Christianity in me was revived: a Christianity

[1] From *On This Island*, by W. H. Auden. Reprinted by permission
of Random House, Inc. Copyright 1937 by Random House, Inc.

that neither abdicates in the face of Mammon, nor proposes concordats with Pontius Pilate, nor offers easy careers to the ambitious, but rather leads to prison, seeing that crucifixion is no longer practised.

As the quotation from Silone pretty directly suggests, the philosophy implicit in these utterances is really that of non-violence, of pacifism: men overcome evil by "the method of the Cross," that is, by refusing to let evil overcome them, refusing to believe that the devils of violence, chicanery, and terrorism can cast out the devil, by being willing to die—not kill—for their faith. But this must logically lead to the renunciation of war, whether international or civil, as Aldous Huxley, of course, has understood. For if there is a "means" utterly beyond the control of those who use it, demanding the betrayal of "the primary human virtues of kindliness, fair dealing, and veracity," which constitutes the crowning instance of what happens when men lose faith in "disciplined love," and resort to hate, "when hatred promises an immediate dividend"—it is war, for whatever purpose it may be waged.

On the other hand, a genuine and thorough-going war-resister policy provides the answer to the dilemma which confronts these writers in the field of practical social action. They cannot accept the inequalities and injustices of the existing social and economic order. Over against it, they must be "revolutionists." But they have come to see that the method which has been employed to achieve "the revolution" leads to disappointment and ultimately despair, and must necessarily do so: "little remains above ground but the tattered slogans of the past," with only "enough magic in them to make them useful to gang leaders." But what is to be done then? The only possible answer is: retreat to the "ivory tower" or else adopt the strategy of war-renunciation which has been set forth in this essay. The system of economic exploitation and imperialism is bound to fall to pieces if it is deprived of its military machine, if it can no longer find an escape from its contradictions in war. If leadership in this direction is given by the intellectuals, there is a real chance that this course will be adopted by large numbers of workers and others who desire basic economic changes, but who have become skeptical of the results likely to be achieved by the method of violence and dictatorship. It would be treason not to insist now that if we seek to gain the world of freedom and justice and brotherhood by the methods of repression, espionage, dictatorship, and war, we shall have the repression, espionage, dictatorship, and war which we practice, and not the fair ends we sought. The way of "disciplined love" may, as Auden suggests, seem in comparison "far too difficult and dull," but it will lead to a moral and spiritual, and therefore thorough, revolution: the means used to achieve it will not completely negate the democracy and fellowship for which, with so much courage and idealism and at such bitter cost, the radical movement has striven in vain.

Chapter VII

Democracy, Police and Pacifism

WE BEGAN BY SUGGESTING THAT THE PROBLEM OF AVOIDING OR ELIMINATING WAR, ORGANIZED VIOLENCE, IS THE CRUCIAL issue today for those who are concerned about the survival of Jewish-Christian religion, of the modern struggle for social justice and of democracy. We then sought to show that the renunciation of war is implied in what is most essential and distinctive in the philosophy of prophetic religion, and that there appears now to be no tenable middle-ground for religious believers between accepting this concept and refusing to have any part in war or reverting to a thorough-going materialism and Machiavellianism. The choice is no longer between totalitarian war and a moderate war which might conceivably come within the traditional theological definition of a "just" war; but between totalitarian war and the renunciation of war. (Whether or not the former alternative was ever a realistic one we need not here discuss.) We next pointed out that if the oppressed and those who sympathize with them seek to achieve social reform or revolution by the method of violence and dictatorship, they also are doomed in advance to defeat. We must find non-violent means to achieve desired social adjustments or we are reduced to futility and despair. We tried also to show that dismantling of the war-machine by refusal of support from labor and progressive forces would itself remove the greatest single obstacle to social change. We must now go on to show that there is a fundamental incompatability between the war-system and organized violence on the one hand and democracy on the other; or to put it positively that there is a necessary connection between pacifism and democracy. So much of what we have already said bears significantly even if indirectly upon the subject of this chapter that we can deal with it in comparatively brief fashion.

For practical purposes we might indeed dispose of the issue of war and democracy by pointing, as has often been done, to the results of the last war to save democracy. That lesson can hardly be pondered too often or too earnestly by the American people. It has been estimated that that war cost, directly and indirectly, thirty million human lives and four hundred billion dollars of wealth. It has been estimated also that for this four hundred billion we could have given to every family in many lands, including Canada, the United States, Great Britain, France, Germany, and Russia, a $2500 house, equipped with $1000 worth of furniture, set on a five acre tract of land. Out of the remainder we could have given to every city of 200,000 inhabitants in all of these countries, a $5,000,000 hospital, a $5,000,000 public library, and a $10,000,000 university. Out of what was then left of the four hundred billion we could pay in perpetuity a salary of a thousand dollars per year to every member of an army of 125,000 nurses and 125,000 teachers. Then we could buy up every inch of land in France and Belgium at 1914 valuation and everything with money value in France and Belgium as of 1914. As a result, we have Hitler at the head of eighty or ninety million people, instead of the Kaiser at the head of sixty million, the progress of democracy has been stopped, and totalitarianism is nearly everywhere on the march. To believe that another more destructive war would somehow save or advance democracy means to be capable of flying in the face of all the evidence—means romanticism to the nth degree. No wonder the press daily quotes the most conservative and restrained leaders warning the American people that we must choose between democracy and war; we cannot have both.

It is, however, necessary to consider the relationship between pacifism and democracy at a somewhat profounder level. There is a sense, of course, in which the assertion so frequently made that democracy or the democratic nations are pacific is absurd and arrantly hypocritical. Devotees of democracy have engaged in ideological wars on its behalf; or at any rate the ideological was one of the factors in some of the wars of the French Revolution and even of the Napoleonic Wars. In recent centuries the so-called democratic powers have conquered vast and rich sections of the globe. Whenever it seemed to them necessary, they did it by means of wars in which they did not hesitate to use such outrageously inhuman methods as England used in the Opium Wars against China or the water-cure to which the United States Army resorted in the Philippines. The contention that these crimes are all in the past and consequently have no bearing on the present international situation would be invalid, even if for the sake of the argument it were granted that democratic nations no longer commit such crimes. These nations still hang on to something like 75 per cent of the earth's vital resources which were obtained by the methods cited; and the crimes of gangsters who hang on by force to an anti-social racket are not in "the past," in spite of the fact that every successful racket takes on some marks of respectability and even conservatism!

Democratic powers have furthermore been so far from pacifist in the sense of relying on anything except armed force that to this very day the preponderance of armament and of means for the production of armaments is in their hands. They thrice promised, in the Covenant of the League of Nations, in the Versailles Treaty, and in a separate memorandum to the Central Powers, to disarm in view of German disarmament. For ten years they hardly made a gesture to carry out their promise. Of the disarmament conference that was finally called H. N. Brailsford, the British publicist, wrote: "Germany was not the only, nor even the chief wrecker. The wrecking was a co-operative enterprise in which the League Powers demonstrated to admiration their capacity for team-work"—in wrecking disarmament. It will be recalled there were also certain American armaments interests who contributed their bit to that result.

It must likewise be granted that the fact that the actual psychology of the democratic peoples has tended to be pacific, averse to standing armies at home, etc., must in considerable measure be ascribed to the fact that they were able to enjoy in comparative peace and security the fruits of their conquests overseas. The wars they were more or less constantly waging were so distant that the home folks could ignore or romanticize them with the aid, for example, of Rudyard Kipling. The bottom pretty much drops out of the familiar contention that the English are "naturally" democrats and peace-lovers whereas the Germans are "naturally" lovers of autocracy and war, when one pauses to consider that "racially" these peoples are of the same stock, and then asks what the German temperament would have been if the Germans had inhabited "the tight little isle" for a few centuries and, per contra, the British psychology if Britishers had lived for centuries in Central Europe, meeting incursions from Asia and, on becoming industrialized, finding that England and France had already staked out claims on most of the desirable spots in Asia and Africa and were not disposed to admit new partners into the corporation.

When, however, all this has been taken into consideration, we are still faced with the fact, which constitutes a factor in the present situation, regardless of how it got there, that democratic peoples do and must constantly boast of their aversion to war; they have regarded freedom from conscription and standing armies as essential bulwarks of democracy; they are, as it were, under a psychological compulsion to believe that they are pacific. They worship peace at any rate as an ideal. They do genuinely shudder at the idea that war should be erected into an ideal, as Mussolini blatantly proclaims. There is a growing reluctance to prepare for war. There is a deep-seated feeling that war and democracy are in their very essence foes; certainly that as things now are, if war stays, democracy is done for.

It is my conviction that all this represents a perfectly

sound intuition on the part of ordinary people and a large part of our elite, that there are profound ties, psychological, philosophical, spiritual, between democracy and pacifism.

Democracy bases itself on the individual, the person, as against the collectivity. The individual is the final reality for whom institutions, including the state, exist. We have already pointed out in our opening chapter that a free, democratic society can be achieved or approximated only if men are capable of making moral decisions and therefore of governing themselves.

So stated, the concept of democracy might appear to represent pure individualism, atomism, and to lead to anarchy. While there has always been the danger of democracy thus eventuating in ultra-individualistic anarchism, it has usually been recognized that individualism and democracy are not synonymous. As the very term suggests, democracy is a "rule," and that is a social concept. Democracy basically means not an aggregation of individuals each going his own way, but a free democratic society.

We must briefly comment on some of the implications of that concept for the argument of this book. In the first place, the concept of authority is often spoken of as an issue between the individual and the state. If the state is given complete and unrestricted authority over the individual, then obviously there is no longer democracy. It is then the state which makes the individuals, not the persons who make the state. If, on the other hand, the individual is regarded purely as an individual, why should his individual judgment, preference, or whim have any standing over against other individuals and more especially over against the state, the collectivity? Should not the individual then submit to the state? It is the fact that democracy seemed to mean simply this elevation of the isolated individual against the state, and the resulting anarchy in thought and action, that has of course given various collectivist systems their standing and appeal for multitudes.

The only way out of this dilemma is to recognize that there is an objective moral law, a moral authority above both the individual and the state, to which both must give obedience; and since it is only the person and not any collectivity which has a conscience and can thus stand in a genuine relationship with this reality, it is the person who has infinite worth and dignity and is indeed qualified to govern himself and therefore to live in a free society.

But this leads to a further explication of the idea. What we have said implies that the human being is an "end in himself," as the philosophers put it, not a mere tool or domestic animal to serve another's ends. His basic need is to be treated as such an "end in himself," to stand in a relationship of confidence, of affection, of fellowship with others, not in a relation of subjection or humiliation or of being ignored. To be able to feel that he is a person, he has to "belong" and he has to be "wanted" somewhere, wanted for himself, not for ulterior purposes or for accidental reasons, such as the color of his skin or his economic status—must "belong" and be "wanted" among his fellows as he is in his own family.

When a man grasps and in the degree that he grasps that this is for him the essence of living, he sees others also as ends, not as his means. That is to say, it is in the very nature of human beings, as human, to constitute free fellowships. Only in such community can they realize themselves. To love and to be loved, to constitute brother-hoods, i.e., democracies, is of the essence of man's nature.

Observe now some of the factors that produce war, that are involved in war-making and the war-system (for whatever purpose it be maintained), and then note how utterly incompatible they are with the very essence of the democratic concept.

One of the concepts upon which war has always openly or covertly been based is that of racism, that the enemy belongs to an "inferior breed." It is the idea on which the wars that accompanied the assumption of "the white man's burden" were based. It is deeply ingrained in the North American attitude toward Latin Americans, which the Latin Americans sense and bitterly resent. It is implicit in our Oriental Exclusion Act and our Jim Crow laws and customs. The British regard this attitude of superiority in the Germans as insufferable, and the Germans reciprocate. The forms of "racism" which are promulgated in Germany are but extreme expressions of an assumption which underlies all war-making, namely, that the enemy is an inferior being with whom normal human relations are impossible—he is savage, he must be kept in subjection "for his own good," he "does not understand any language except that of force." It may be noted that where the conflict of economic interests passes into actual class-war, capitalist and worker are similarly convinced that the other side is composed not of human beings but of monsters or inferior beings: the capitalist a degenerate and sadist because of luxury and the habit of power; the worker a creature of low mentality, defective energy and low moral habits who is at the bottom of the social scale because that is where he belongs. It is doubtful whether human beings can fight for any length of time unless they make themselves believe in the essential inferiority of the enemy.

This whole idea clashes head-on with the democratic concept. Democracy, as we have seen, rests its case on the person, the human being as human, not on this or that breed or class. If, for example, we adopt the idea that Americans are a superior breed who must rule other breeds "for their own benefit," the bottom drops out of the democratic concept. If there are inferior breeds in Asia or Africa, on what ground will you argue that dark-skinned Americans are not inferior to white, or of course white to black in the estimation of the latter? Furthermore, why is it not then plausible to assume that the present economic and political rulers constitute a superior class? Once you abandon the position that it is man as such who has moral dignity and infinite worth, only brute force and cunning can settle such questions.

As might be expected, therefore, rejection of democracy in the internal life of a people always goes hand in hand with its rejection in their foreign relations. We have not clearly seen that as democrats we could not consistently wage open or covert warfare against "inferior" peoples, against whom our own superiority had to be guarded, because we have not been genuine democrats at home, have treated negroes, Jews, Catholics, Communists at home as inferiors who could legitimately be put down, "kept in their place" as the revealing phrase has it, by force of one kind or another.

Democracies can engage in conquest because they are not imbued with the democratic spirit at home. On the other hand, in the degree that democracies engage in imperialistic and war-like practices abroad, they tend to adopt more non-democratic, authoritarian practices at home. Fortunate circumstances which it is not necessary here to discuss concealed that fact during much of the nineteenth century from the English and American peoples, but it is plain that those days are gone. All minority groups in a nation which encourage or fail to combat trends to imperialism and war are inevitably storing up trouble for themselves. They cannot fall in with practices of racism and authoritarianism abroad and then expect that somehow another view of life will prevail at home. At home, since they are the "inferiors," the "dangerous elements," they will be on the receiving end of the violence. Minority groups who are hot for another war should bear this in mind. If the United States gets involved in war, there will when it is over be a revulsion on the part of our people. There will have to be a scapegoat, and inevitably the minority groups will be cast in that rôle.

Another concept of basic significance in connection with modern war is that of nationalism. According to this concept as held even in democratic countries, the state is really a sacred collectivity, an absolute as against other nations. It has none but its own interests to serve. The idea of mutuality, or fellowship, is excluded. There is no law to which it is subject. But how can a state be an absolute existing only for its own perpetuation and the pursuit of its own interests, as over against other states, and then be an entirely different entity as against its own citizens? Obviously it cannot be for long, or in more than a very limited degree.

What if this autonomous, sacred, super-individual entity which is "my nation" is threatened by another such entity? Must it not then demand the absolute allegiance of its own citizens? And if so, in what sense do they have any autonomous, independent existence over against this "Leviathan"? Once again we see that a nation cannot be one thing in its internal and another in its external life. A genuinely democratic nation which would be a society of free individuals co-operating for the common good would find it a moral impossibility to treat peoples of other nations as subjects or slaves. It would be as impossible for such a people to settle external differences by war as to deal with internal offenses by the method of lynching. The reason why so-called democracies can wage war and engage in exploitation of other peoples is that they are not democracies but economic oligarchies. Both the economic contradictions and the divided soul, the split personality, of the pseudo-democracies keep them forever shrinking from war and yet forever tangled in war.

On the other hand, in the degree that "democracies" engage in imperialism and war, their own people lose more of their liberties. Today in the era of totalitarian war, the contradiction between nationalism and democracy, always implicit, has become clear and explicit.

This is why there is no solution, not even an approximate political compromise likely to hold up for any length of time, for the problem of the Conscientious Objector, so long as the nationalistic concept of the state prevails. Genuine democracy of course requires of its citizens that they be independent spirits, genuinely free and conscientious souls who recognize a "higher law." What if it turns about and seeks to coerce their consciences into committing what they regard as the most outrageous and criminal acts? It is certainly true that the conscientious objector must consider seriously his obligations to his fellows arising out of his inextricable involvement in the economic, political, and cultural order with them; and this precisely because he is a conscientious, and not a conscienceless, objector. But the real burden of proof, when it comes to the attempt to coerce conscience, is not on him but on the state, if that state claims to be democratic. It is betraying the basic concept of democracy and undermining the very foundations of a free society when it tries to compel its most sensitive and useful citizens—and incidentally those with the highest I Q's, as the War Department records of the last war reveal—to violate their most sacred and profound convictions.

Of course, in modern totalitarian war complete repression of all opposition and criticism is involved. Thus, here again the contradiction between democracy and nationalism, always implicit, stands out in all its nakedness. Mankind must choose between democracy and nationalism; it cannot have both. And if it wants democracy, it will also have to abandon war and find non-violent means for solving conflicts, for it is no longer possible to wage war without making the nationalistic state absolute.

We have tried to show that there is an inherent contradiction between the idea of democracy and the concepts of racism and nationalism on which the modern war-system largely rests. It remains to point out that there is the same contradiction between the idea of democracy and that of violence as a means for settling differences.

Within the nation the democratic citizen will not submit to external power and authority, not even, in the final analysis, that of the state. It is not, according to the democratic concept, force that holds society together. It is the mutual advantage both in a material and spiritual sense that society offers men, the fact that it is in "community," in free association, that men find meaningful and satisfying life. There was, in the thinking of the founding fathers, no need of an army to police a people who are free to discuss and to settle differences in a democratic fashion, and whose freedom to do so is not illusory but genuine, because they are also free in their economic relationship—free farmers cultivating their own land, free artisans wielding their own tools in their own shops, or employees who are free to make their own contracts of employment with employers of their own choice. As there is no need for any to wield power over others, so too there are none worthy to exercise power over others, no families or other groups set apart for that purpose. Nor are there any whom power does not corrupt, so that all possible restraint is put even upon those to whom power is temporarily entrusted on behalf of the group. Political issues under such a set-up are settled by discussion and the recording of the popular will following discussion.

It is of the very essence of the democratic way of life that society is thought of as held together not by violence but by the justice which is embodied in the organization of any given society and the human community, the fellowship, which it makes possible. The resort to compulsion and violence is in itself an abandonment of democratic process. There is a desperate need in these days of crisis for democracy to learn that we cannot ride two horses going in opposite directions: we must, conservatives and radicals alike, take our chance with the democratic process and refrain from resorting to violence, or otherwise honestly face the fact that we are operating on a non-democratic or anti-democratic basis. On the other hand, when violence breaks out, the logical conclusion is not that "human nature is like that" and that this violence "must" be met by counter-violence on the part of society; but rather that there must be some essential injustice, i.e., covert violence, denial of community, in the basic arrangement of that society. Intelligent people will accordingly not resort to or join in violence which will settle nothing and probably aggravate the situation; they will seek to establish justice and true community. As they do that, they will discover that others are not "naturally" violent any more than they are themselves, and that essential fair dealing begets fair dealing, and love is the "natural" response to love.

At this point the question is sure to be raised: But how about the police? Would not any civilized community sink rapidly into chaos if the hand of the police were taken off? Does this not prove that in the show-down it is force that holds society together? Would the pacifist dispense with police force? And if not, then what logical ground has he for objecting to such "police measures" as society may have to take in order to put Adolf Hitler where he can no longer go about "as a roaring lion seeking whom he may devour"? The problems here raised are important enough to warrant at least a cursory examination.

The first point to be made is that there is a big pragmatic

difference between war and the use of police power in any of the usual senses of that term, and that therefore, in spite of logical or philosophical issues that may be raised, people may well reject war as a method for achieving security or justice, while not completely rejecting the use of force by the police. Certainly it seems quite illogical for non-pacifists, who are constantly insisting that we must often be satisfied with "relative" justice, that we must be governed in daily life by practical political considerations as to what can be achieved in a given situation, to turn on pacifists and insist that the latter must be absolutists—either reject all use of physical force or continue to support war.

Police function under a reign of law. It is, furthermore, a law which is on the whole accepted by society, by those who live under it, and this because it embodies an approximation to justice, because men find mutual advantage under the set-up, some degree of real "community" is achieved. That is why there are police and not an army. That it is this factor which gives the police their "power" becomes clear the moment one reflects how few the police are compared to the population or how impossible it is to enforce an unpopular law. The policeman is not the legislator, executive, judge, and executioner rolled into one. He brings the person he has arrested into court where that person has numerous and well-defined rights. It is the business of the police to isolate offenders as carefully as possible from non-offenders, and to limit to the minimum possible the amount of injury done even to criminals. The police force of one city does not go to war against the police force of a sister city. In civilized societies the aim of law, police, and courts is not to destroy offenders, but to place them under reforming and redemptive agencies.

Among nations there is no society in the proper sense of the term; each claims absolute autonomy. When attempts have been made to organize a society of nations, as in the case of the Wilsonian League, they have proved abortive because nations did not abate their sovereignty and because the real if not avowed aim was not to establish economic equity but to perpetuate the power and privileges of some nations against others. Thus there was no law in the proper sense of the term and no courts fitted to determine guilt when crucial issues arose. Under the circumstances, what was called collective security amounted to collective insecurity. Armies do not seek to reduce or eliminate violence. They do not distinguish between innocent and guilty; not a few experts believe that it is the non-combatants who are least safe in modern war. The victims of war are placed forever beyond the reach of reforming and redemptive agencies on earth. Besides, what evidence is there that modern war can settle anything, can defend any one or any thing of value, that it means anything but mass suicide?

Turning to another phase of the problem under discussion, it appears on closer inspection that the terms "police power" or "force" in connection with police activities are used at different times to designate very different things. Sometimes the police function as "guardians of the public peace" in a clearly defined and, on the whole, legitimate sense; often the police force functions as an army in disguise. The point may perhaps be made clear by an illustration from the field of industrial conflict.

In England if on a Saturday night a few men get into a fight, for the reasons that get men into brawls on Saturday night, the police appear on the scene and perform the function of guardians of the public peace. The men actually engaged in "the private war" are with a good deal of care isolated from those who are not and, if the affair has been sufficiently serious, are placed under arrest. In due time, the processes of law having been observed, the offenders will be sentenced in court. In the United States if the same sort of thing happens on a Saturday night essentially the same procedure will be followed.

If in England a similar breach of the peace occurs in connection with an industrial dispute, on a picket line, for example, the police will follow the same procedure as if this breach of the peace had nothing to do with a strike situation. The police are not armed; they will take pains to separate those actually engaged in fighting from others; they will use a minimum of violence. When the case comes into court the sentence imposed will not differ from the sentence ordinarily imposed for such a disturbance. In the United States, on the contrary, a very different policy is often followed in strike situations by the agents of the state, of government. When a disturbance occurs the police, who are armed, who have given evidences of fear or of truculence and hostility toward the strikers, who may be working in close collaboration with private guards or even agents provocateurs hired by the company involved in the dispute, attack in force and indiscriminately. They make no serious effort to distinguish between those who are actually engaged in physical combat and those who are not. A whole area will be "cleared" by use of clubs and perhaps tear gas on anyone within range. When the offenders get into court, the sentence is likely to be more severe than it would have been for a similar breach of the peace not associated with an industrial dispute. Quite possibly an injunction will be issued against the union involved, so that all its activities, no matter how peaceful and legal they may be, are handicapped.

I am satisfied as a result of many years of observation and first-hand participation in strikes that in this contrast in procedure we have in large measure the explanation of why there is likely to be more violence in any little strike of a hundred bricklayers or automobile workers in this country than in a British general strike involving three or four million people. In one type of case the police genuinely represent the community of which all those involved are in real sense a part. They are the embodiment and guardians of a social set-up, a law, which brings mutual advantage to all, which represents an approximation to justice and is therefore in the main tolerated and even cherished. It is not, therefore, the physical force the police may be able to exert with which alone those who have lost their heads must cope, but public opinion, the whole pressure of the community from which by their violence they have as it were sought to separate themselves. What the police do in such cases is to isolate the violence. Their coming has a calming effect and makes it possible for healing influences to begin to operate upon the offenders as well as others. In the other type of case, still too distressingly frequent in this country, there is to begin with a grave inequity in the situation. There are unjustifiable differences in income; workers are not free to organize to deal with these grievances; employers have been using open or covert violence, perhaps through discharging workers who took the initiative in forming a union and thus threatening them and their families with starvation, and through the use of labor spies. There is, therefore, to that extent, no community but denial of community, a state of war. The police then enter the situation not as the representatives of the community but of one side in the war. Often they are quite conscious of this and make no effort whatever to conceal it: they are proud to represent "the better elements." (There are, of course, instances where the shoe is on the other foot and "the better elements" are the workers on whose behalf the "law-enforcement" agencies fight against "wicked absentee landlords" or "cockroach manufacturers," as small employers are called in the textile and garment trades.) But whether or not the police are clearly conscious of it, they do in fact fight on one side in the war. They add to the violence in the situation, and have been known to provoke it in order to discredit strikers. Instead of isolating the element of violence and seeing to it that it has no bearing on the settlement of the controversy between employer and employee, they throw the force of the state on one side and against the other, so that it is the violence and not the merits of the issue that determines the outcome.

Only, the pacifist proceeds to point out, in this case as in every other, war settles nothing. War only leads to more war, violence begets violence. The original grievance about wages and purchasing power is not settled, the resort to violence having diverted attention from that, and the situation becomes worse in that respect. The strikers may yield for the moment to superior force, but they have become embittered, and have further lost faith in our institutions. The class conflict is intensified. So-called "police protection" has to be increased. Presently soldiers have to be used openly in industrial conflicts, so that it is now plain for all to see that we have war on our hands and that the "public peace" is in no sense being "guarded," but constantly jeopardized. A little later, as has happened in many European lands already, the nation is split into opposing camps and, whichever camp wins, totalitarianism and violence are enthroned and democracy—which, as we have been trying to establish, cannot be mixed with violence— lies violated and dead. To complete the picture, we need only point out that these internal conflicts and tensions contribute in various ways to produce conflicts with other nations, again substantiating the contention that violence simply begets violence. The only possible way to break this vicious process at any point is to renounce violence, to abandon all dependence upon it, and to take steps to deal with the underlying issue. As soon as that is done, community is made possible, the constructive good-will on which alone any human association and more especially democracy can stand, has been made operative.

There are those who are prepared to grant that there is much to be said for this non-violent approach in the industrial conflict, but who ask, "Surely you cannot deal with the gangster problem in this fashion?" I think we can and must, and that only in the measure that we abandon faith in violence and apply constructive good-will to this social problem also shall we find any solution. Gangsterism also grows out of the lack of community, the denial of justice, in our social organism. Every social worker can tell the story of housing conditions, lack of sunshine and fresh air, lack of wholesome recreational facilities in the slum areas from which many gangsters come. We live under an economy where not a few make "easy money" while millions of sober, industrious citizens, including four or five million young people, have lost whatever savings they may have had, have had to give up the homes they had tried to buy, are without jobs. It is by no means always easy to say with respect to businesses regarded as legitimate how much the element of public service obtains and how much the element of racketeering, making as much profit as possible at the expense of the public, figures. In international affairs our civilization is constantly giving youth a lesson on a world-scale of gun-play as the final arbiter of human destiny, and nations are constantly training young men by the million in the use of guns!

To dream that under such conditions such phenomena as gangsterism will not develop is indeed childish. And what evidence have we that war in this field any more than in any other achieves even limited and temporary good? It is, of course, true that a particular set of gangsters can be killed off and some forms of gangsterism may be eliminated. Where a permanent change for the better takes place it will be found, we are confident, that internal changes in a business or union rather than killing off or jailing individuals are basically responsible. For the rest, so-called lawlessness takes other forms temporarily. But do we find that we are able to reduce our police forces, that our jail population falls off, that we can close up some of our mental hospitals, that life in "civilized" communities grows more quiet and secure? To ask the question is to answer it. In so far as any actual progress is being made, it is the result of dealing with social causes such as bad housing (badly retarded because we think it more urgent to build battleships) and of new methods in criminology and psychiatry all of which tend away from faith in repression and violence and toward dependence on non-violence and constructive good-will.

In order to avoid any misunderstanding, let me make it clear at this point that in explaining as I see them the causes of some of our social problems, criticizing the policies of government and its agents, and professing complete lack of confidence in violence as a way of dealing with these social evils, I am not for a moment justifying or condoning the violence of strikers, for example, not to mention gangsters. I can see no moral justification for the use of violence, though willingly agreeing that there are cases where resistance to evil and injustice even by violent means is an ethically nobler attitude than cowardly or passive acquiescence in evil. My experience in the labor and radical movements, furthermore, convinced me that violence is self-defeating when workers resort to it, quite as the open and covert violence used by employers or agents of the state is self-defeating. The oppressed will make surer and faster progress if they eschew violence and depend, as they do mainly depend in their organizing and strike activities, on their solidarity, courage, capacity for suffering and sacrifice, and on non-co-operation where injustice becomes extreme. No saying in all history has, in my opinion, been validated more consistently in all lands and times and in all the relationships of life than Jesus', which may be paraphrased in the words: Put up your sword into its place, for they that take the sword—no matter how great the provocation, how ideal the end, how apparently certain the victory—they that take the sword shall perish by the sword.

There are two other questions which frequently arise in connection with the discussion of police force to which brief reference may properly be made here. In the first place, the pacifist is often told that he receives the protection of his community's police force, as of his country's army and navy, for his business, his property, his own life and that of his dear ones. He is the beneficiary of the "force" or "violence" thus exerted; therefore, he may not wash his hands of it, nor refuse to join "the forces of law-and-order" when need arises. If this means that the pacifist is tied "in the bundle of life" with his fellow-men, that he is inextricably involved in the social system and also therefore implicated in its evil, and that he may not ever take the position of one who draws his skirts around him and thanks God that he is not as other men are, this is, as we have stated in an earlier chapter, a valid point and can hardly be too often emphasized. The pacifist is certainly also under the positive obligation to make certain that he refuses so far as possible to benefit by open or covert violence, that in his personal living he refrains as far as possible from enjoying privileges which others may not share and which come to him out of a system based on inequity and violence, and that he is exerting his utmost efforts to exemplify another way of life and bring in a better society. As we have also already pointed out, innumerable times, most ticklish problems arise in the daily working out of this attitude, problems for which there are no neat and universally applicable answers. Each individual or group must arrive at its own answer from day to day with God's help by the use of intelligence and creative imagination. It will always be possible to ask the pacifist uncomfortable questions, and the same holds true for the non-pacifist. If the result is that both are saved from arrogance and complacency, God be praised.

The pacifist will, of course, be grateful for all the blessings that come to him from living in an orderly society, belonging to a community, local, national, or international. He will therefore discharge gladly all those duties of citizenship which he can conscientiously discharge. But when the pacifist is asked to give countenance or support which he might withhold to the various forms of violence we have been discussing, on the ground that they provide him with his own security, he will ask leave to differ. He will point to the arguments which we have been setting forth which seem to him to prove that these various agencies of violence employed by the state, whether by the police when they operate as a disguised army, or by armies and navies themselves do not provide him or his dear ones or his fellow-citizens safety and security but insecurity and peril, peril so dire that with all the vast "protective" and "defensive" organs we have built ourselves, no one, whether he looks at the internal social situation or at his country's foreign relationships, feels that he has any assurance as to what the morrow may bring forth. All these agencies of violence, the pacifist holds, are means which divert our attention from the actual causes of insecurity and keep us from exercising our intelligence and good-will to provide true security. In order, therefore, that some day he and his fellows may live in a safer and more lovely world, he must continue to bear witness against violence in all its forms and in so far as possible must dissociate himself from their maintenance and employment.

The second matter to which we referred a moment ago as needing brief consideration is that of "international police force." We have already pointed out that between police power and the use to which armies are put by nations claiming complete national autonomy, acting therefore as their own respective legislators, executives, judges, and executioners, there is simply no analogy whatever.

We have abundant proof that when a political federation is built upon economic arrangements genuinely beneficial to the parties involved, it is held together by the mutual benefits derived. Armies are not needed. Only those arrangements which benefit one group at the expense of another require force for their maintenance. The federation of American colonies, the North German Customs Union which held together states as different as Prussia and Bavaria, the great progress toward a solution of the nationalities problem in the Soviet Union, are illustrations that readily suggest themselves of our contention that where there is mutual advantage, an approximation to justice, armies are not needed to hold groups together.

For the rest, the analogy of police power in connection with the relations between a world-state and its constituent parts seems to me almost completely worthless and usually extremely dangerous. Suppose that national armies have been abolished and that such military forces as survive have been placed under the control of a League of Nations, which recruits them from various nations, as the United States recruits them from its various states. Then suppose that an economic issue develops and that some powerful nation (or, as is more likely to be the case, combination of nations) feels itself sufficiently aggrieved to be willing to fight, as the southern states did in the 1860's. Will not the struggle that ensues be war? And will it make any difference that each side argues in effect that it is simply using police power against gangsters? Civil wars are notoriously bitter and destructive. As H. M. Swanwick in her book *Collective Insecurity* suggests, "A League War, however lofty its motive," would probably in no important respect "differ from any other modern war." And might not an international army, actually capable in a military sense of "enforcing" peace, become the most terrible instrument of tyranny the world has yet known?

Despite all this, most pacifists would, I suppose, talk to their brethren of the "collective security" school in some such terms as these:

If the leading imperialist nations in the present set-up will stop thinking of themselves in Pharisaic fashion as policemen over against imperialist powers cast in the rôle of gangsters; if they will renounce and undo "Versailles"; if they will abandon the armament race; if they will take steps toward solving the economic issues which bedevil the world and toward setting up a genuine world-organization—if they thus get off the road on which they have been traveling to perdition and get onto an entirely new road, the benefits accruing under such a "New Deal" will be a cement strong enough to hold the peoples of the earth together without resort to the horrible persuasion of war. It will be much better if, having entered on this new road, the nations of the world burn the bridge of force behind them. If some of you still think you must have something you call an "international police force," we shall argue against this mistaken policy in all democratic ways that may be open, just as we oppose the war-equipment and the war-policies of the nations of which we are now citizens. If you undertake to make war with your "police force," regardless of what you call that war, we shall be conscientious objectors to it. But we shall gladly admit that the rôle of violence in international life has shrunk enormously; and in all the constructive activities of a world-organization built on such essentially sound lines we shall gladly and loyally participate.

At a number of points in recent pages our argument has proceeded on the assumption that there is a significant ethical distinction between the use of police force, in the stricter sense of the term, in order to preserve the peace of the community, and "violence" in various forms. Obviously this raises the question of whether the thorough-going pacifist can ever approve of any use of "force," whether the latter can ever be compatible with the love-ethic of the New Testament, "the way of the Cross," the faith in non-violence.

Discussions of this question sometimes appear to start with the assumption that it is possible for human beings not to exert influence or pressure on each other. Of course, a moment's reflection would show that if it were possible it would not be desirable, certainly not from the pacifist's point of view. For this idea implies that human beings are thought of as self-contained atoms never touching each other; it is an extremely individualistic, atomistic conception. The religious pacifist conception of man is, on the contrary, a profoundly social one. To the pacifist "the neighbor" must be loved because he is, quite literally, "the other self," whom one can no more think of wanting to injure, to put in the wrong, to destroy than one can think of wanting to do these things to oneself, but whom one can no more escape either than one can escape oneself.

The mere fact of existence means to influence, to impress oneself in various ways upon another and to limit his possible choices. A few years ago certain educators and parents talked in most fantastic terms about not "coercing" children, leaving them alone, absolutely free to express themselves, apparently quite oblivious of the fact that in pursuance of this theory they were creating one type of environment for the child to grow up in and very definitely excluding it thereby from another, and all without the child's being in a position to say or do anything about it, though his future might largely be determined and perhaps blighted by these attitudes and actions of parents and educators. When Tolstoy pursued his policy of nearly complete non-resistance, he was certainly presenting his wife and children with facts which they did not freely choose and yet had to reckon with. The conscientious objector in war-time cannot avoid doing the same. There is, as these illustrations suggest, no guarantee either that we may not, however unwillingly, inflict suffering on others no matter how non-violent our course may be. We cannot vote, we cannot expound our view to others, we cannot buy this article instead of that from the first merchant instead of the second without thus exerting pressure upon others.

Another observation that these illustrations suggest is that there is no clear ground for saying that direct application of physical force to another is necessarily evil, whereas psychological pressure is good. Psychological compulsion may be of the most vicious sort both in its motivation and in its effects.

What then are the tests? So far as I can see, they are the ones discussed in an earlier chapter. We must, for one thing, inquire into the inner motivation for actions. If the motivation is hate, the desire to injure or punish or humiliate, revenge, indifference to the person of another, insensitivity to his condition and need, it is an evil motivation. If the motivation is to heal, to help, to forgive, to redeem, it is good. But, on the other hand, actions must be tested by their results in so far as we can foresee and evaluate them. If the result that you foresee from a given course is the most constructive, the most productive of good for all involved in the situation—the offender also being accepted fully as a person, a child of God—then that course is good, it is your duty to pursue it. As we have already pointed out, we do not believe that participation in war can meet those tests. We can, on the other hand, imagine that physical force might be used in the exercise of police power, by private citizens in preventing a drink-crazed man from injuring himself and others, etc., in such a way as to meet the above-mentioned tests and to be compatible with the ethic of love and non-violence. It might be added that it is also quite possible to use "non-violent techniques" in a spirit of violence and hate. A plain soldier doing his duty as he sees it and advancing no moral pretensions may be nearer the Kingdom of God than a self-righteous and censorious non-resister. What is right, the expression of love, in a given situation must in the final analysis be decided by each person for himself.

Having said this, we must, however, immediately add that resort to physical force is always fraught with danger; it is perhaps always a sign of weakness, not of strength. On the other hand, most of us have not even begun to explore the possibilities of what Gandhi sometimes calls "soul-force" and also Satyagraha, which means literally insistence on truth, the possibilities of love. Gandhi himself is, of course, an illustration of the point. The whole British Empire trembles when it appears that the little man "with no shirt at all" may die in the course of a fast which he undertakes to protest against a wrong which that Empire refuses to right!

How inadequate physical force may prove at any moment in the presence of greater force. But a spirit which is not seeking its own, which has no fear, which is calm and collected, which has no desire to injure any one, which stretches out its hands in trust and love toward others—such a spirit does not put forth those war-like bodily signals of aggression or defense which other human beings and even animals so swiftly sense and toward which they react in hate or terror. On the contrary, such a spirit creates that environment of peace for which the troubled humans who are driven to violence by the conflict and tension in their own souls so desperately long. The presence of the man who is himself whole makes them whole, and so the weapons drop from their hands. Those who are dealing with the mentally troubled are increasingly aware of these facts. To glance at an entirely different field for a moment, the unarmed Quakers in Pennsylvania were safe from attack by Indians for sixty years while in all the other colonies armed whites suffered massacres. Then one day a couple of Quakers, a little afraid, and influenced by the example of other white men, took guns with them to their work some distance from their cabin. The Indians concluded that the Quakers must be contemplating an attack on them, decided that the best defense was an offensive, and promptly killed the Quakers.

The hours a man spends in prayer, cleansing his soul from self-will and fear and drawing into his weak and parched soul the infinite Power and Love which is at the heart of this universe, will do infinitely more to prepare him to guard the innocent from attack than training for physical combat whether with fists or guns. In an emergency a man might not be able to reach his gun or it might jam. But God and a heart at peace with itself are always within reach. Those who profess Christ certainly ought to ponder Paul's counsel about the Christian's weapons in Ephesians VI. "Be strong in the Lord and in the power of his might. Put on the whole armor of God!" And of what does that consist? The girdle of truth, the breast plate of righteousness, feet shod "with the preparation of the Gospel of peace," the shield of faith, the helmet of salvation, "the sword of the Spirit which is the word of God," and prayer! And this is the proper armory because, as Paul says, "our wrestling is not against flesh and blood" but against spiritual forces. Struggle is basically spiritual and spiritual weapons alone prevail in the end. Richard B. Gregg, in his standard work, *The Power of Non-Violence*, has discussed this matter from the psychological angle and gives many instances illustrating the effectiveness of non-violent techniques.

We have taken a somewhat lengthy excursion into the consideration of the function of police power, etc., in our effort to show that it is mutual interest, biological, material, and spiritual, and not external force which binds human beings together; that democracy pre-eminently embodies this idea of "community" in which and for which human beings live; that democracy is necessarily abandoned and destroyed the moment violence enters into the political and economic process; that, in other words, there is a necessary connection between democracy and non-violence. We must now round out the argument of this chapter.

In the case of the two other concepts which enter importantly into the modern war-making process and which are antipathetic to democracy, viz., racism and nationalism, we pointed out that a nation cannot be one thing in its internal life and another in its external relations. If, for example, autocratic and jingoistic tendencies are manifest in a nation's dealings with other countries, these prove to be the outward expression of tyrannical and exploiting forces in its internal life and in turn strengthen and confirm such internal evils. On the other hand, imperialism in a nation's foreign policy always involves certain forms of injustice and oppression at home, and eventually imposes the crushing burden of militarism and totalitarian war on its citizens. People who make subjects of others will themselves be subjects, and will soon wake up with horror to the realization of that fact.

The same holds true with respect to violence. In the degree that violence is the rule in the relations between classes and interests within the nation, the nation will be war-like in its attitudes toward other states. In part this will be because violence in class relationships means that economic relationships are unsound but that the people refuse to face the difficulty realistically and remove it. The effort is then made to find an escape from poverty and distress by foreign conquest. In part the problem is psychological. Where community does not exist, where men are in the unnatural state of bitterness and hostility toward each other, they must either "repent," as Jesus and the prophets put it, the contending groups each recognizing its guilt and therefore able to address itself to a realistic solution of the problem, or like the individual with a divided personality, they must project the blame on another nation and relieve the intolerable inner tension by seeking to destroy it. That the situation is utterly irrational is illustrated by the shifting alliances among the nations in a war crisis. The enemy who must be devoured today may be your ally tomorrow, and then the foe to be annihilated will be your friend of the day before, the point being that there must be some one on whom to wreak the inner tension, and it does not matter who it is.

Fascism is a name for a régime based almost exclusively on naked violence, on the complete suppression of internal liberty. The shocking abnormalities of such a régime, the fact that there are quite precisely manifestations of insanity associated with it, is eloquent testimony to the religious view that men are children of God and brothers of one another, that they were made for freedom and love, and the absence of these is intolerable and drives them mad. But observe that a Fascist state, i.e., a state which approximates the perfect embodiment of violence in its internal life, is also a war-state, it must constantly approximate perfect violence in its external relationships also, it must be fighting all the time until it destroys itself—unless it comes back to its senses by renouncing violence. The same of course holds good for the brand of communism which obtains in Russia today.

But the idea that the way to end this state of violence is by war, i.e., by violence, is also irrational, for the process we have been describing works also from the opposite end. In the degree that a nation is at war within, we have said, it will be at war without; Fascism is therefore another name for war. But it is equally true, and now plain for all to see, that in the degree that a nation gives itself to violence and war in its external relations, it must put its internal life on a war-basis; must cut down the social services; must destroy civil liberties; must regiment industry, agriculture, labor, education, religion; must cease to regard the enemy as human, instill hate for him, elevate ruthlessness into a major virtue, condone and presently glory in terrorism—must adopt Fascism. Fascism is another name for war; war is another name for Fascism. As the last war has already suggested, you cannot teach men by the millions to shoot and then expect that at eleven o'clock on a misty November morning you can quietly tell them to go home—life is now

overcome evil, and that the structure of the universe is such that there must be another alternative, a "good" which the creative imagination and the humble spirit may find and which can indeed overcome evil. Finally he will subject all proposed solutions to careful scrutiny and choose the one which, so far as he can foresee, will produce constructive results.

With such an approach we looked out upon the European scene in those closing months of the year of our Lord 1939 which witnessed the twenty-first anniversary of the armistice which brought World War I to a stop, and some weeks before that date witnessed the outbreak of World War II. The present war is getting under way slowly. Save for the episode of the Polish invasion it has none of the characteristics of the *Blitzkrieg*—lightning war— which had been looked for. It is the war nobody seems to want. There is nowhere any enthusiasm for it. There seems to be something elemental, deep-seated, about the shrinking of the masses from war. They sense perhaps, as J. Middleton Murry in particular has suggested, that war is mass-suicide. Therefore the very instinct of self-preservation, which in other epochs led the individual to sacrifice himself with some satisfaction or even elation for the clan or nation, now moves men to draw back from war which now will not save but inevitably destroy the nation, yes, western civilization itself. Governments quite obviously also shrink from the plunge into unrestricted warfare. They see or sense that, unless war is ruled out, every nation faces impossible, diabolical dilemmas.

Let us for a moment dwell upon that fact. If a real war gets under way in Europe, it may end in one of three ways

—a victory for Germany, or a victory for the Allies, or a stalemate of exhaustion. Victory in either case will mean winning in somewhat the same sense as the Allies won in the last war. Before analyzing these alternatives we may glance at two possibilities in case there is an early end to military operations. One is that rather than face the consequences of general war now, a "peace" is made on the basis of the status quo, recognizing German and Russian advances in Poland and the Baltic and for the rest leaving things substantially as they are. That will mean reverting to the "Munich" policy of pseudo-appeasement at the expense of small countries. It is hardly conceivable that the British and French would permit their governments to adopt such a course. There is always something to be said for a situation where men are not actually engaged in wholesale slaughter; there remains the chance that before the guns go off again, sanity may return and steps toward a genuine peace be taken. But there would be no more substantial hope in reversion to "Munich" than there was in "Munich" to begin with. (Giving away what does not belong to you and then hurrying home to speed up your armament program so that you can take it back in six months, or at least avoid giving away anything of your own, never did spell appeasement or peace in the intelligent pacifist's dictionary!)

The other possibility to which I alluded a moment ago is that fear of bolshevism may lead France and Britain to make peace with some régime in Germany which will join them in an anti-Russian policy; but this also would be returning in essentials to the "Munich" line and also holds out no substantial and permanent hope for peace.

Let us assume then what at the moment of writing seems likely: that the war gradually or not so gradually becomes more intense and draws in more countries and that the outcome is what may be described as a victory for Germany; Germany will write the document that others have to sign. What will that mean?

Germany will not be able to win without the active collaboration of Russia, and support or benevolent neutrality on the part of Italy and Japan. It is quite possible that to date (December, 1939) Stalin is simply living day by day, keeping Germany fighting with France and Britain, thus avoiding the trap which he believes, and not without reason, French and British conservatives set for him, viz., that he should get involved in a war with Hitler in which Russia and Germany would exhaust each other to the advantage of French and British imperialism; and instead he is watching the western European powers weakening each other to Russia's advantage. In the meantime, he would take advantage presumably of the preoccupation of the western powers with their own worries to extend Russian power into the Baltic, the Balkans, the Near East, the Far East, wherever he might find "a soft spot." Obviously even such a prospect poses to the Allies the question of whether they can possibly have anything to gain from continuance of a war on such terms!

It may well be, however, that the same forces which drove Hitler and Stalin into each other's arms at the beginning of the war—an event which came as an utter surprise to many, but which profounder students had long foretold—that these same forces may keep them locked in that embrace and even drive them closer together. It may be, in other words, that there is in process of formation a vast bloc of revisionist, totalitarian, militaristic, anti-democratic, anti-Christian (and equally anti-Jewish, at least so far as religion is concerned) powers stretching from the Rhine to the Pacific. It would be the aim of such a combination to put an end to French and British hegemony in Europe, Asia, and Africa, to re-draw the map of the world in wholesale fashion, and to substitute a radically new culture and religion for those which now prevail in the Orient and Occident alike. No one in his senses will, it seems to me, claim that such a prospect is an attractive one.

Not that this Russo-German combination would, as some Americans seem to fear, launch an expedition to invade the United States the day after the "peace" was signed in Europe. We have only to ask ourselves just how England and France could have managed such an invasion, if they had desired it, at the conclusion of the last war to see how silly is the assumption that after an even more exhausting war any one would be in a position soon to make such a move. Experts have often pointed out that such an invading expedition would require a million men and that there do not happen to be ships enough in all the world to transport that many men with necessary supplies and equipment. To those who fear Japan we may remark that it would take the same kind of forces to effect a successful invasion from that side and the trip across the Pacific takes quite a bit longer than that across the Atlantic.

But over all of Europe east of the Rhine after such a Hitler victory some form of "communazism," a debased bolshevism robbed of all the earlier idealism of the communist movement, would reign, a régime in which Christians would be hunted as of old in Roman catacombs. Furthermore, much the same kind of régime would be imposed on France and Britain, will for that matter be accepted and even sought by the French and British people, or what is left of them. They will exhibit all those reactions of a defeated people which Russians and Germans showed at the end of the last war. They will turn on their present rulers, and repudiate the way of life which has ended in such a debacle, believing that democracy was indeed an idle and a bad dream.

It is the fear of this horrible disaster which leads many people in the United States to say that we must give all the material help we can to France and Britain, and will lead them tomorrow to say that we must go in and fight on the side of those nations in order to save civilization and religion. Already, since a war for democracy still has a bitter sound in the ears of the American people and since it is so palpable that when war comes democracy must go, the truly "holy war" to save the last precious remnants of civilization and of Christian faith is being preached by some.

Very well then, let us suppose we go in and that once again as the result of our intervention France and Britain win. What then? Will the French and British empires then be strengthened so that they can impose a "righteous" peace and keep Germany and the rest of Europe amenable to living under a Franco-British peace? These same nations won the last war, but although victors, they had lost strength and prestige both absolutely and relatively to the United States, Russia, and the Asiatic peoples. It was not possible to keep in subjection a Germany which was licked, whose navy was sunk, whose army was disbanded, whose economy was nearly ruined by inflation. Granted that Germany may be much weaker after an exhausting war, will France and Britain be stronger than after the last one?

What will happen in defeated Germany? There will be another Woodrow Wilson—sometimes it seems that an old disciple of Wilson's now in the President's chair pictures himself in the rôle—to set forth another idealistic Fourteen Points as the basis for an armistice. There will also be another Clemenceau and Lloyd George. Personally honest and sincere, perhaps they will "accept" this basis for peace. Actually, however, they will be compelled by their own past course and by war-drunk public opinion to say: "After having had to go through this thing a second time, after the terrific cost of this war, in the name of our boys who died in battle and our women and babies who were bombed to death by the Huns, we must exclude these savages forever from civilized society, we must make it impossible for Germany ever to raise her head again. . . ." Alas, they will not be able to offer a decent peace then, if they cannot bring themselves to it now.

Even if they did, what chance is there that the Germans would believe and accept it, after what happened the last time, when there were also promising features about the peace, such as a new League of Nations, to which republican Germany eagerly sought admission only to be kept cooling her heels for years on the outside? Defeated Germany will be in a position similar to that of Russia at the close of the last war, except that in a highly industrialized nation after a more destructive war the disorganization and terror must necessarily be much more extreme. The same kind of thing will inevitably happen as happened in Russia, only this time there will be none of the idealism about it that marked the early years of the Russian Revolution. It will be a naked military dictatorship. What chance will there be that French and British armies of occupation could police such a situation? What chance even that they could get food to keep them alive?

We must go on from that point to ask what the French and British people are likely to do as they go back to "peaceful" existence and attempt to eat the fruits of their "victory"—finding as they did before the "victory" turning to ashes in the mouths of the returned soldiers; finding no revenue coming from India, which will hardly remain a vassal through a long war; finding, as before, that the only victor in terms of power politics and prestige is Uncle Shylock from across the water, who came in late after cornering the gold and the trade, and who got off relatively easy? How much physical, economic, spiritual energy will there be left among these peoples to stem the tide of militaristic totalitarianism?

In other words, there are no victors and vanquished in any important sense in modern war. It makes no difference, therefore, which side "wins." The same is obviously true if a long war ends in a stalemate of exhaustion, with no one even able to claim a victory. In any case, the vultures will descend to tear what remains of the prostrate body of European civilization.

The Christian or prophetic conscience, as we remarked in an earlier chapter, is often sensitive to the evil in a social arrangement before men in general become sensitive. Those who share the concern about the evil bear witness against it. In the beginning and perhaps for a long time they will be a small minority. But the time comes when such changes in the political and economic scene, such advances in culture occur as to make the institution in question clearly unfit for survival. Then—after a more or less violent struggle on part of its beneficiaries, or more correctly those who still can make themselves believe that they benefit from it—the institution is removed. Thenceforth the general conscience of mankind agrees in condemning it, and men regard with horror any proposal to restore it.

Something like that has been the history of the institution of chattel slavery, for example. The whole contention of this book is that we have arrived at such a final stage with regard to the method and institution of war, the stage when the whole technological, economic, political, cultural situation is such that the traditional attitude of, for example, the Society of Friends toward war must be universally adopted or mankind must suffer a colossal reverse. There is no moral or rational justification left for war, any war. There is no way to meet the situation which we have analyzed except the renunciation of war. This seemingly idealistic, by which men usually mean unrealistic, solution has become practical politics. "The way of the Cross" which seemed foolishness to men proves once more to be divine wisdom.

There is a policy based upon the philosophy of non-violence which we have sought to portray which offers the nations a way out of the hell in which they find themselves. It is for the nations which were the "victors" in the last war, which know by bitter experience how disastrous every victory is, which failed utterly to use their victory for the purposes which they had professed—the whole story of the Versailles peace and its aftermath has been told many times and will not be rehearsed here—it is for these nations to offer now to such nations as Germany, Italy, and Japan a just and decent peace.

What would be the elements of such a peace? In a world in which there is violent disagreement on almost everything, this is one question to which nearly everybody gives the same answer. A peace that would be a real peace and a stable one would have to include the following points:

1. There must be drastic reduction of armaments all around, looking toward the complete elimination of national war establishments; and the dismantling of the armament economies of the various nations which are gradually but rapidly choking all other economic life.

2. The people of all nations must have equal access to raw materials. In the United States, except for certain reactionary tendencies to set up trade barriers between states again, the citizens of New York or Arizona have access to the resources of Pennsylvania and Ohio on the same terms as the citizens of the latter states. The fact that we have thus had a vast free trading area here is one of the chief reasons for the prosperity which through the years this country has enjoyed. The same situation must come to obtain among the nations of the earth. This will require, among other things, gradual but drastic lowering of tariff barriers and stabilization of currencies, so that they may be used to promote trade and co-operation, not,

as is now the case, as a weapon in economic war by one nation against another.

3. A substantial start must be made on the basis of sound economic adjustments, such as we have just suggested, toward genuine federal world-government along the tested lines of our own federal union. Perhaps the first step would be the formation of a United States of Europe, long recognized as a necessity by far-sighted European statesmen, although the Versailles settlement was unfortunately based upon the opposite idea of the fragmentation or Balkanization of great sections of that unhappy continent. Also in this field internationalization of control of colonies must be provided for.

It is not the purpose of this book to enter into a discussion of the details of working out such proposals as these. That there are immense difficulties and complexities we are well aware. We are also convinced that men and women who can meet the organizational problems involved in carrying on a great modern industry, or such a nation as the United States, or a modern war, are quite capable of meeting the economic and technical problems connected with the organization of world-peace. It is not the difficulties in this field that are holding back peace on earth. Lack of true understanding of the facts about international relations and the causes of war, the real or supposed interests of various economic and political groupings, and the absence of the faith and will-power necessary to break out of the chains with which the nations are today bound, these are the supreme obstacles to world-peace. One or two observations relating to these matters then will suffice for our purpose.

It is necessary to emphasize the importance of correcting underlying economic ills such as the present one-sided control of natural resources and food supplies and embodying sounder economic arrangements at the very outset in the peace-structure. Seemingly fair, democratic, idealistic political arrangements will simply be covert means for perpetuating economic injustice unless this is done. In large measure the nullification of the political advance represented in the League of Nations was due to this factor: the linking of the League with the economic subordination of Germany, the fragmentation of Europe, the suicidal tariff policies, etc., which were a part of the Versailles structure. A political organization must always embody what is at the time a progressive and mutually beneficial economic base or the former will be hopelessly unstable. In the estimation of the present writer Clarence Streit's *Union Now* plan errs at this vital point, which is a great misfortune in view of the highly desirable features of his proposal, such as the emphasis on the necessity of nations abating their claims to complete autonomy. Bringing, in the main, "the North Atlantic democracies" together in a League tied up with the economic inequities which we have mentioned led to disaster; this was inevitably so because these economic arrangements were a denial of democracy at the most vital point. Bringing these same "North Atlantic democracies" together in a still more attractive looking political set-up called a Union, which is still tied up with the economic inequity of the fact that they are the "have" nations, will lead to disaster again. A nation like Germany must be offered a square economic deal first; then she will be able to believe that political democracy can work as it could not on the basis of Versailles.

This matter of the "have" nations consenting to basic changes in the status quo is often spoken of in terms of sacrifices these nations must be willing to make. There is a sense in which this is correct. Certainly no peace can be had on terms of throwing small nations to the dictators while hanging on to your own colonies and exclusive markets. But the old law that he who seeks his life shall lose it, but he who is willing to lose it shall find it is directly applicable here. England would grant India independence as part of such a peace as we propose, and that might be regarded as a sacrifice. But how long will England be able to hold on to India in any case? England can try to hold on to her colonies rather than "sacrifice" them in a peace which involves international control of colonies; but what is she gaining if she must then live in a world where every generation she must engage in deadly conflict with certain other nations? Examples could of course be multiplied indefinitely. On the other hand, if such "sacrifice" as this were made, then Indians might welcome trade with England, world-trade generally might be revived from the paralysis which has gripped it since 1914, the intolerable burden of armaments would be lifted from the backs of toiling men. Verily if the peoples had but faith to follow Christ's way we should "receive a hundredfold now in this time, houses and brethren and sisters and mothers and children and lands," all which will otherwise perish, as we wail and gnash our teeth, in the hell of war.

One more observation on the peace terms which we have mentioned. Though, as we have said, there is general agreement that these terms are desirable and indeed the only ones on which a stable peace can be erected, the feeling is often expressed that it is expecting a good deal to ask the Powers to take down tariff walls, disarm, etc. That is in a sense true. But if the point has been reached where the patient must undergo a major operation or die, it is no good to put on a mustard-plaster or to tell the patient that the operation is a serious matter and leave it at that. The thing to do is to operate. Surely there are few who would claim that the world does not have to face a major operation today. There is, however, another figure that may be used in describing what must be done to avoid disaster. It is not proposed that the world should wake up on some bright morning and instantaneously disarm, tear down all tariff walls, assemble the parliament of man. The trouble with the world is that it has been running headlong straight away from all these things and as a result is on the brink of hell and may pitch over it. What is needed is simply that we shall turn square around and begin to move in the other direction. Even small genuine steps in the new direction will swiftly alleviate the situation and surely bring us out into a new world eventually.

Now whenever in the United States the proposal is made that the "victors" in the last war should now offer such peace terms as we have stated to Germany and other unsatisfied and so-called dynamic Powers, two questions are invariably asked. Would Hitler accept? And if he did, could he be trusted to keep any agreements he might make?

If we go back to our description of the religious pacifist approach, we shall immediately recognize that those questions assume that the beam is in the other fellow's eye; we shall at once be on guard therefore and shall ask whether there may not be a beam in our own eye which needs removing. As soon as we do that, we shall realize that there are prior or at least parallel questions which must be asked. An offer cannot be accepted or rejected until it is made. We must ask, therefore, whether there is any chance that Chamberlain and Daladier and Roosevelt will offer to write a decent peace. And if they did and international agreements were made on that basis, could they be trusted to keep their word any more than Lloyd George and Clemenceau and American statesmen did after the last war?

At the date of writing France and Britain have persistently refused to state war aims or peace terms in any but the vaguest terms. As late as three months after the British declaration of war a poll taken by the British Institute of Public Opinion revealed that over half of those who had an opinion on the matter, and nearly one half of all those polled, believed that it was imperative that the British government should clarify its war aims; only 12 per cent of all those polled were against the proposal. And this in the very midst of a war which, we are told, is a war to save democracy, civilization and religion. Over half of the British people, according to an unusually trustworthy source, have the gravest doubts about that!

On the very day when the result of this poll was made public Lord Halifax, the British Foreign Minister, trying to meet insistent demands for a definition of war aims, said in the House of Lords: "The primary aim of being engaged in war is to win it; and the first purpose we must have is the defeat of those—who obliged us to take arms," i.e., of the boys who started the fight! But this means in effect: "We are out to win the war. When that has been accomplished, we shall indicate by our actions, if not by verbal confession, for what imperialist aims and secret treaties we have really been fighting—what we promised Hitler when we tried to use him against Stalin; what we promised those well-known democracies Poland, Rumania, and Turkey for their help; what we are offering Mussolini in order to induce him and the Italian Emperor of Ethiopia to join the champions of democracy and peace; why we go to war against Hitler for invading Poland but let it be known that we have no intention of ever asking Stalin to give back the Polish territory he took over; and what it is we are offering Stalin if, as we fondly hope, we can induce him to 'double-cross' Hitler as he once 'double-crossed' Chamberlain."

Is this to suggest that Chamberlain and Daladier are monsters whose motives are beneath contempt? No, it is suggesting that they are caught in the toils of a complex and desperate situation which they are trying to work out by the old method of meeting violence with violence and evil with evil, and that as long as they do that, no matter how fine their motives, they will only add to the evil and get themselves and their people mired more deeply in disaster; and it is suggesting that the same thing may be true of Hitler and Stalin, who certainly also have sought to bring self-respect and glory to their people by the world's ancient methods and today also face desperate dilemmas.

We are saying that the ancient religious insight is again vindicated: the war is not between angels and devils. It is between, on one hand, a group of nations satisfied with a status quo which is vastly to their advantage, a status quo which they achieved by a series of wars including the last one, in which they have refused to make a single basic change, and which they are armed to the teeth to maintain even if that means plunging the world into another war (though they would like nothing better than to be left in peace holding on to their superior position and extending such merciful concessions as they please to other nations, even as they did to Germany, for example, in the Versailles settlement), and on the other hand, a group of nations equally armed to the teeth and determined to smash the status quo and no longer accept an inferior status, even if that means plunging the world into another war. To put it another way, it is a war between one misguided group of God's children called Englishmen and Frenchmen and Americans and another group of misguided children of God named Germans and Russians and Japanese.

"But is not a régime such as the French or British, in which some freedom still exists and Christian churches may function openly, preferable to a Hitler or Stalin régime?" Yes, God knows. But it does not follow that we must go to war on the side of France and Britain. We need to know whether it is democracy or imperialist interests and secret treaties for which they are fighting. We need to know whether, even if the governments of France and England were engaged in an approximately pure war for democracy, war is a means by which democracy can be protected. Deep down in his heart does any one believe that it is? Does any one believe that from a serious and prolonged war anything but disaster can come for all we hold dear? "Then shall be great tribulation, such as hath not been from the beginning of the world until now."

Since, whatever construction one may put on recent history, Germany is also a grievous offender against the laws of God and man and has resorted to violence as a means of realizing her purposes, is it not as much her duty as that of France, Britain, and the United States to take the initiative in offering to substitute a policy of conciliation and fair-dealing? Of course it is, and of course the policy of violence will prove disastrous to her as to other nations. It is the duty of pacifists in Germany to condemn their country's sins and mistakes and to bear witness to a better way. Let us remember that there are those in Germany who are doing that very thing. Not a few are in concentration camps, ready to make the same sacrifices for their convictions that American or British pacifists are ready to make, and some German conscientious objectors have been shot for refusing military service.

Our business in America is, however, primarily that of recognizing and repenting of the evil in ourselves and our associates among the nations. We need not point out again that there is ample ground for this take-the-beam-out-of-your-own-eye attitude in Jesus and all the great religious spirits. There is equal warrant for it, as we have indicated in an earlier chapter, in the teaching of such a man as Lenin. What he was constantly saying to the Russian workers was, in effect: "The enemy against which you are fighting is militarism and imperialism, not Germany or France or Japan. If you get involved in war-preparations and war against these other countries, then you are the agents of Russian militarism and imperialism. When the war, in which multitudes of you and your brothers in other lands will have lost your lives, comes to an end, militarism and imperialism will not be defeated, but only some particular militarist and imperialist nation. Meantime another nation or bloc of nations will have been strengthened relatively, if not absolutely; militarism and imperialism will remain to curse mankind. Therefore," Lenin continued, "you must attack militarism and imperialism where you can really reach them, and that is at home and not on the other side of the border. Make it impossible for your own agencies of violence to function, for your own nation to bring death to its own and other peoples in war. Then you will indeed be dealing a death-blow to militarism and imperialism. The armaments of one nation find their justification in the armaments of the neighbor nation. The whole edifice of imperialism will cave in if at some one point the masses will just withdraw support from it. Your refusal to go on with war will have revolutionary repercussions in other lands where the workers will be encouraged to throw off their shackles. . . ." Those who remember the six or seven years following 1917 when Lenin's policies in a measure prevailed in Russia will agree that the deed of the Russian workers in laying down their arms and walking out on the imperialist war had indeed tremendous effects on the governments and peoples of other lands.

We may conclude the discussion of this point by emphasizing that in a very real sense a greater responsibility for initiating a new international régime of conciliation and fair dealing rests with nations like the United States and the western European democracies. "This is so," Mr. John

Foster Dulles puts it in that penetrating study of international relations, *War, Peace and Change,* "if for no other reason than that the peoples of such countries can be expected to possess better judgment and act more normally and rationally than those which are emotionally aroused in consequence of what they have conceived to be undue restraint." As far back as November, 1915, D. H. Lawrence raised a similar point when in a letter to a friend he pointed out that if with a sullen, evil soul a mother provokes an evil mood in a child, the mother cannot permit the situation to continue until the child destroys himself and perhaps her too. She must at a certain point "yield to the paroxysm of the child, which passes away swiftly when the opposition is removed. . . . This is not yielding to the child—this is knowing beyond the child's knowledge." Germany, he suggested was the child, perhaps we should now say the adolescent of Europe, evil but not all evil; no child ever is. "The good will not be long in coming all over Europe if we trust it in ourselves."

That sentence brings us back to the two crucial questions we were asking a few pages back. Is there any hope, in the first place, that Britain and France, backed by the United States, will "trust the good" in themselves and offer now a decent peace along the lines we have described? There is, we believe, a chance though it may be dangerous to be too optimistic. There is a chance because, as we pointed out in our analysis of the possible outcomes of the war, a point has been reached where the child in sullen, evil mood is on the point of destroying itself and the mother. Whichever way a serious war ends so far as outward appearance goes, in reality it will end in doom for all the nations, and certainly will be the end of all the present governments. The world's wisdom having thus proved foolishness, they may turn to the foolishness of forgiveness, love, and truth as the only wisdom left for mankind.

Suppose Chamberlain and Daladier made such an offer, would Hitler accept? The answer is that there is about as much or as little chance that Hitler will accept as that the others will make the offer. (Incidentally, those who are so certain that Hitler would not accept a really decent peace must answer the question why such an offer has never been made, since it would obviously be such a fine chance to put him finally "on the spot," not with other nations, which does not mean much, but with his own people.) There is a chance, in other words, that Hitler or his colleagues or both may see the true state of things, may realize that it is the end of him too if the decision is for war without restriction, and may not be sleeping too comfortably by the side of Joseph Stalin!

Certainly if such a peace offer as we have advocated were made—with some evidence of its genuineness—neither Hitler nor any one else in Germany who refused the offer and then tried to keep the Germans fighting would in my opinion have any more chance of survival than the proverbial snowball in an overheated place. There is not the slightest evidence that given the choice between a genuine new deal in international affairs and suicide, the Germans would choose the latter.

If then, to ask our second question, Chamberlain and Daladier made such an offer, could they be trusted to carry out the peace arrangements that would ensue? The answer, we believe, is in the affirmative. In the first place, if the "satisfied" democratic nations could once achieve the moral height of confessing that they have a full share of responsibility for the mess in which the nations find themselves and basing their actions at a peace conference on that ground, that attitude of mind and will would carry over into the execution of the plans thus made, as surely as the Versailles mentality and ethics carried over into the years after 1919. In the second place, now that the peoples of Europe have stood on the brink of hell and have been staring over the edge, if they were once demobilized it would take a long time for any one to induce them to resume the process of mobilization. Similarly, if the various national economies were gotten off their present artificial and insane armament basis, and on a normal foundation, it would take a very long time to persuade any one to resort to the armaments boom racket again. Finally, the hope of peaceful progress and improvement of living conditions which would result from such a peace would bring release and joy to the peoples, such as millions believed Wilson was bringing in 1919. This would keep the peoples from desiring war or supporting any leader who wanted to go back to the old way.

Could Hitler, or whoever else was in command in Germany, be trusted, if such a peace were accepted, to carry out its terms? It is almost like asking whether a thirsty man can be trusted to take a drink. German leadership could be trusted on the same grounds we have mentioned in speaking of Allied leadership: because they would then be the prisoners of good-will, fair-dealing, justice, and of the longing for peace of their own peoples and other peoples, as Hitler is today the prisoner of the past follies of the Allies, the war-mentality he has helped to create, his own war-machine—and of one Joseph Stalin!

Two other points in the political program of American pacifists in the present crisis require brief comment. The first has to do with the rôle of the United States in world affairs; the second with the problem of the weaker nations.

For reasons, in some instances alluded to in earlier chapters, which have been adequately discussed in other books and in periodical literature and which we do not repeat here, pacifists believe that it would be disastrous for other nations as well as the United States if we should get involved in the present European war. But the religious pacifist with his faith in the Fatherhood of God and the Brotherhood of Man is not and cannot be an isolationist. He condemns, on the one hand, the policy of American interventionism, economic and military, in the wars of other nations. He condemns equally our traditional policy of isolation from peaceful co-operation with other nations for the economic and political ordering of the world. American refusal to enter the League of Nations might have been justified on the ground that the League was from the outset a worthless instrument for peace because it was tied to the economic and political ineptitudes and injustices of Versailles; but as a matter of fact we remained out because we wanted to be perfectly free to determine our own destiny as a completely autonomous nation which would not resign a particle of its sovereignty. That is isolationism which is highly immoral and, as is apt to be the case with anything that violates the moral law, impractical: it simply means that since we have taken no steps to co-operate in organizing an interdependent world for peace, we feel impelled periodically to intervene in war in order to protect and advance our real or alleged interests.

The United States as by far the richest and mightiest nation on earth must participate fully in peaceful efforts to organize peace. That brings up first of all the basic requirement of self-criticism and repentance. We must recognize that we too are a war-like and imperialist nation. In order to provide ourselves *lebensraum*, as Hitler puts it, we brutally drove the Indians from their lands, shamelessly breaking over two hundred treaties in the process. We pushed our power out into the West Indies, across the Pacific to Hawaii and the Philippines. We assert that we have special interests in the whole North and South American hemisphere and are sole judges of what other nations may do there, though we can see no sense in Germany's claim to a sphere of special influence in a small section of Europe. We have invaded little nations such as Mexico, Haiti, Nicaragua, and have kept our soldiers in them for years. When we felt we needed it for purposes of naval strategy and national security we seized Panama, the key spot in the western hemisphere. Similar considerations lead the Russians to want the part of Finnish soil from which their second city, Leningrad, can be threatened, and threatened much more directly than any one could threaten us from Panama. It is true that we did not often have to wage bloody wars in order to achieve these things, because our neighbors were usually too small to offer even a gesture of resistance and there were no other great powers on which they might rely for help or which might egg them on to fight us. But when we felt we needed to, as in the Philippines, we did not hesitate to wage a three years' war on a small people and with very brutal means. And we are armed and arming to the teeth in order to hang on to our privileged position, arming at a rate which is certainly not necessary for defense of our soil and which is accordingly frankly regarded as provocative by Japan, a much weaker and more poorly armed nation. Do not imagine that I am unaware of other and finer aspects of American life. A "sweet land of liberty" it is. But the imperialist aspect which I have pointed to is a part of our history and being as a nation, and we must see that. Other nations whom we are inclined to condemn utterly also have fine and noble attributes, and we must recognize that also.

We must make our contribution to a noble and stable peace first of all then by stopping our own imperialist practices. We should, for example, grant the Philippines unqualified independence or, if they prefer, full statehood. We should be willing to internationalize control of the Panama Canal. We should go on to participate in lowering tariff barriers all around, in a planned and orderly manner, of course, so that presently all peoples may have access to the resources of any individual state on the same terms as its own inhabitants. Those who may be terrified at such a prospect will do well to recall that our present tariff and immigration policies, which helped to put the screws on south and east European peoples and so to prepare another war, quite obviously did not bring us prosperity either. They may consider also how much more desperate our situation would be if the United States were divided into a dozen nations waging tariff and currency wars against each other. With our present technological equipment mankind could move on to undreamed of prosperity if we could muster the imagination, intelligence, and courage to do now on a world-scale what the founding fathers did on a continental scale a century and a half ago.

The United States must participate also, of course, in an honest movement to reduce and presently to cut out armaments altogether. We certainly have no moral right to ask any other nation to move in that direction until we are ready to join in. The pacifist, however, unblushingly proposes that the United States should show some real imagination, as well as courage and Christian faith—or perhaps common sense is all that is required—by scrapping its armaments and purchasing genuine instead of fake security by offering to spend the billions we now spend on armament in the rehabilitation of European economic life. It is by now clear surely that piling up armaments means piling up insecurity and terror. We fear that the example of disarmament would not be followed. How can men be so sure of that? The example of armament certainly is copied with a vengeance. I believe with all my soul that the embattled peoples of the earth looking at each other like savage witch-dancers through gas-masks are waiting for a nation that would have the sublime horse sense, the divine foolishness, to break the evil spell that is on mankind, lay down its arms, and say: "Boys, this thing has gone too far; I'm going home to work and live and love; and the next time I get restless and want some excitement, I'm going fishing or to see the Marx Brothers in a movie or maybe even to church." Uncle Sam and his Yankees ought to be capable of that if anyone is!

The fear of a policy of unilateral disarmament is largely based on the assumption that if a nation were disarmed, it would be the simplest thing in the world for some dictator to lead an army to conquer and devastate it. The fact is that the leaders of all countries have their hands full trying to induce their people to wage war today when there is an army facing them across the frontier, and there is therefore some show of reason for the contention that if they do not attack they will be attacked. Even under these circumstances there is not a single big nation which can depend on volunteers to wage war. Men have to be conscripted, and then they have to be kept in line by means of a huge propaganda—i.e., falsification—machine. With all that, the rulers have a hard time keeping the men from fraternizing in the front line. The abhorrence on the part of the masses of "the dirty business of killing" is everywhere apparent. How likely is it that men released from this nightmare, from fear of attack, could be led to slaughter a helpless population?

Suppose a disarmed nation were "conquered." Then the conqueror must reap the fruits of his conquest. But it has been demonstrated that under modern conditi... at any rate this can no longer be done. Germany was conqu...ed. When the Ruhr was invaded a few years after the armistice in an effort by France to get some good out of her victory, all prostrate Germany could do was to offer passive resistance. Even so France had to give up the effort. The only way to get milk out of a cow is to permit her to eat and become strong, France discovered. That is, the only way in our interdependent economy to get anything out of another people is to help them grow rich so that they will be good customers. The German example may serve to suggest also that to subdue the spirit of a people is as difficult as to realize economic benefits from their conquest—a lesson Germany will have rubbed in next by those laws of God that may sometimes grind slowly but that grind exceedingly sure. At any rate, when war with present-day weapons is likely to mean virtual extermination of whole peoples, one can understand why Bertrand Russell said a couple of years ago that he would prefer a temporary conquest of England by Hitler to war, since live Englishmen with their farms and industries still existent could be trusted not to become slaves, had at the very least a chance left to regain freedom; whereas dead Englishmen were dead and those who remained alive after a real war, whether they belonged to a conquering or a conquered nation, would be the victims of a shattered economy and the slaves of a debased and debasing military dictatorship.

Nor is it the case that people or movements which are in a military sense disarmed have no means of self-defense and of resistance to evil. The Jews who are still here, while many martial peoples have vanished, are a witness to that. The Christian church, which began as a sect, often bitterly persecuted, of people who would not bow to Cæsar's image or serve in his armies, are a witness to that. Such instances can be multiplied almost indefinitely. With much less effort than is required to put a nation on a war-basis, it could be organized to meet, confuse, and rout an invader with non-violent non-co-operation, as Dr. Jessie Wallace Hughan, building upon some suggestions of Bertrand Russell, has clearly demonstrated in a pamphlet entitled

If We Should Be Invaded. And Gandhi in India is demonstrating that there are non-violent techniques that can be effectively used in the struggle for political independence and economic and social justice. The British government could hardly have been more terrified at the thought of defeat in battle or in a revolutionary war than it was a few months ago at the thought that Gandhi might die in the midst of a fast conducted in protest against an unjust policy of that government but amidst protestations on the part of the frail leader of good-will toward the members of the government and the British people. An illuminating, scientific study of these techniques, commended by such leading American sociologists as Professors Robert M. MacIver and Robert S. Lynd of Columbia University has been recently published by a former associate of Gandhi, K. Shridharani, under the title *War Without Violence*.

There are those who go a long way, if not the entire distance, with the pacifist in his analysis of the conflicting imperialisms of the great powers and the catastrophe that is bound to overtake western civilization if the war-system is not smashed. They are almost ready to entertain the idea that disarmament might actually be a wise move on the part of one or more of these powers. They are, however, deeply stirred by the attack on small nations such as Ethiopia, Austria, Czechoslovakia, China, Albania, Poland, and now Finland. With some show of irritation often they ask what a pacifist has to say to such "utterly unjustifiable and unnecessary violence," and how he would meet it except by force of arms.

No one will condone or justify these attacks, least of all pacifists who are opposed to all war. I have already declared that resistance even by violent means against injustice and oppression may indicate a better moral state on the part of an individual or social group than apathetic or cowardly acquiescence. But a great deal more needs to be said.

In the first place, the cases cited do not constitute a proof that the non-violent way having been fairly tried has been a failure. Not one of the countries cited has ever disarmed, put its faith in non-violence, and tried to work out techniques for defense on that basis. No modern nation has ever fully espoused this philosophy, though Denmark came very near doing it a few years ago, which may or may not have anything to do with the fact that for all her proximity to Germany Denmark has been safer from attack than several of her neighbors. In recent years all of these countries have to the extent of their resources imitated their stronger neighbors and have gone in for increased armament. It is permissible to argue that in the world as at present constituted this was a sensible thing for them to do, but not in the same breath to argue that they furnish the proof that the method of disarmament and pacifism will not work: obviously they never tried that method.

From what might be described as a worldly-wise viewpoint, the question might be raised whether it would not pay for the small nations precisely to get out of the war-business completely and take their chances on that basis. For if their safety depends in the last analysis on military might, they can obviously never be safe. The big nations will always have the best of it in that case. A small nation will enjoy even temporary security only because of some tacit or open support from a big Power, and the big Powers have, alas, often demonstrated how little their word to a small nation counts when their own interests are involved.

That suggests another point which must be kept in mind in dealing with this problem of the small nation under attack. It is never possible to take the case of Big Power A versus Little Power X and isolate it in space or time. It must be seen in its setting in world history and contemporary conditions. Thus regarded, it always appears that A really attacks X as a means of getting at another Big Power B or a bloc of Big Powers. Likely as not B has advantageous trade relations with X from which A has been excluded; or B has advanced money to X for its armament as B's means of offense or defense against A; X may have had its boundaries determined largely in order to deprive A of strategic military positions which it might have used against B. There is not a single situation of Big Power versus poor Little Power in recent years in which such considerations as these have not been vital and decisive. It is necessary to name but a few of them. Czechoslovakia's boundaries were drawn against the advice of Thomas Masaryk so as to give France and England through their ally a means of keeping Germany down. For the same purpose France encouraged the huge Skoda munitions works and a big armament program in Czechoslovakia and financed the Polish dictatorship long before there was any Hitlerism in Germany. When Austria earnestly desired *anschluss* with liberal Germany in order to save her economic life, France by threat of force prevented it for her own imperialistic reasons. It is quite impossible to understand Japanese aggression in China except in the light of English, French,

German, Russian aggressions over a long period, the exclusion of Japan from British Empire markets, the exclusion of Japanese from Australia, the seizure of the Philippines by the United States. So we might go on until volumes had been filled.

The only way really to help the small nations, which under present conditions are doomed to lead a precarious existence at the mercy of their larger neighbors and periodically to constitute the battlefields on which the bigger nations fight their wars, is to put an end to the aggression which is the essence of imperialistic militarism and which is all the time being practiced, openly or in disguised fashion, by all the great Powers including the United States. The way to do that, as we have already described, is to begin at home, for us Americans to withdraw all support from the war-making activities of our own government.

Certainly we should not sell munitions to any power which is at a particular moment aggressive. But if we sell to one belligerent and not to another, we are taking sides in a war. We ought rather, therefore, to refuse to sell munitions or materials likely to be used for war-purposes to any one at any time. There is no reason to think that another American expedition, on behalf of a poor little nation will produce any more good for us or any one else than did our intervention on behalf of poor little Belgium. If we should go to war to free Finland from Russia, why not go to war to free three hundred and fifty millions in India from British rule? It always turns out that our sympathies for the woes of a particular little nation were used to get us into a specific war—while we failed to be as deeply moved by the woes of another small people—because propaganda misled us as to the facts and because our own imperialist concerns or native economic lords required that particular war.

In the interests of realism it must be said too that the little nation which happens to enlist our sympathies is never the stainless virgin we imagine her to be, and certainly will be even less pure after having been drawn into the vortex of modern war. The fact that Chiang Kai-shek was not many years ago responsible for the slaughter of millions of Chinese peasants and workers, members of trade unions and peasant associations, is never mentioned today by radicals and progressives who a few years ago denounced him as a bloodthirsty military dictator. They were not discriminating in their vilification then; but neither are they discriminating in their whitewashing now. The struggle between the rising Chinese capitalist class and Japanese capitalists is a factor in the present Japanese-Chinese war and such incidents as the massacre of workers and peasants by their own military are as much a factor in that kind of struggle as in international warfare in which, for variety, the plain people of opposing nations spend a few months or years in massacring each other. During that international war the soldiers on each side accept as leaders those native lords who a little while before were persecuting and exploiting them but who now laud them as patriotic and truly pious defenders of the common fatherland. When will the masses see that the reasons given for all wars are rationalizations and cry out: "We are through with war, all through with all war"?

If, to pursue this line of thought just one step further, the Chinese should win the present war, it would in all probability be with help from one or more big Powers. China would have to pay for that help. It would mean that China would be drawn into the vortex of Power-politics, of chronic world war. In any event China would win only by developing a powerful military machine. Then China and Japan would face each other as France and Germany, for example, have faced each other and periodically fought in Europe until both are now threatened with annihilation. Is that a hopeful prospect for the Chinese people, or the Japanese for that matter? Yes, I am aware that there are many who firmly believe that a Chinese military machine will be something new under the sun. And I grieve that so often it seems to be true that "the only thing men learn from history is that men learn nothing from history." And I am inclined to agree with those who have said that the greatest catastrophe of the war in the Orient is that the Chinese, who for centuries were inclined to follow a near-pacifist course and who built and maintained, be it noted, during those centuries the oldest stable civilization and in some respects the noblest in history, are now embracing the unhappy example of western, shall we say Christian, militarism.

Once again let us say it: This is not condoning Japanese war on China, it is not blinding ourselves to the heroism of the Chinese people, nor being callous to their stupendous suffering. We have simply come by another path to the old message which now shouts to men from every housetop in all the earth: "Put up your sword into its place; for they that take the sword shall perish by the sword."

When his own nation, whether it be the United States or India or Britain or China or Japan or Germany or Russia, gets involved in war, the pacifist still refuses to fight, rendering such service as he may to relieve suffering; to keep the ordinary processes of life such as raising food, building homes, educating and rearing children going; to keep down the fires of hate, bitterness, and lies; to bring about a decent peace; to keep some faith in love and God and beauty and decency alive in human hearts. But he refuses to fight or to render any service under military orders which he believes contributes to the military effort of his own government—and he is prepared to take the consequences. He has his personal reasons. He has to "save his soul" in a sense. He would have to deny himself, to deny Christ as he understands Him, if he were to kill. There is a tendency on the part of some to ridicule pacifists on this score. But the question, "What shall a man give in exchange for his soul?" was asked by a very high authority. Each human being has to answer it. The same people who criticise pacifists for concern about their inner integrity are likely to applaud the lad who cries: "Why, I should lose my soul, all self-respect, if I did not answer my country's call!" We say to that lad and his friends that he must indeed go to war so long as that is his conviction; but he should have at least equal respect for one who believes that he too has heard "a trumpet sound from the hid battlements of eternity" and who looking up is impelled to reply: "His Name I know and what His trumpet saith." It is always a sad day for society, especially for democratic society when it can find no place but the concentration camp or the cross for such men.

This is, as we have tried to show, more true than ever in view of the nature of war with modern weapons and under modern conditions. As Mr. Milton S. Mayer, assistant to the president of the University of Chicago, has recently said: "Society may make many demands upon me, so long as it keeps me out of the cave. It may take my property. It may take my life. But when it puts me back into the cave I must say, politely but firmly, to hell with society. My ancestors were cannibals without benefit of parliaments."

But the pacifist's personal religious or humanitarian reasons for refusing to participate in war are closely linked with what he regards as valid social and political reasons. He is not, as we have already intimated, impressed with the suggestion that the fact that his country decides to go to war necessarily makes it a just one. No one would be so rash as to claim that for past wars: why should it necessarily be true of his country's present and future wars? Besides, the assumption that one's own nation is waging a just war is always associated with the idea that the other nation is waging an unjust war, and that if its citizens were not fools or barbarians or insane they would refuse to take part in such a monstrous crime. Common sense, not to mention Christian convictions about the common sonship of men to a common Father, suggests that it is likely that he is misled in fighting these "enemies" as they are in fighting him; that it is about time some one acted on that assumption and, even if there were not an immediate response, kept on acting on that assumption, stayed out of the crazy death-dance of war, confident that presently others and still others would realize that there was an escape, namely, as Mr. Mayer put it, to "sit this one out."

Nor is the pacifist impressed with the argument that he

has received the protection of his nation's armament and that his countrymen at war are fighting for the safety of him and his dear ones. He does not for a moment question that many of them sincerely believe this to be the case, just as in all sincerity men have burned heretics at the stake for the greater glory of God and the salvation of heretics' souls. He believes, however, that all the evidence calmly weighed shows that they are mistaken. Armaments are a source of insecurity. War for whatever purpose waged in these days creates more insecurity both while it lasts and as its inevitable aftermath.

The pacifist believes therefore that at the present time the most positive thing he can do for the safety and the material and moral well-being of his countrymen and of all mankind is absolutely to refuse support to any war. That conviction was eloquently and passionately expressed recently in a private letter to the author by one who has earned his right to speak on the subject—Evan W. Thomas, M.D., who was perhaps the most widely known of the American Conscientious Objectors during the last war, and whose work over many years in a special field of medicine is gladly recognized by all who know of it as constructive civic service of the finest sort. I am grateful to my friend Dr. Thomas for permission to quote here a portion of that letter.

Young people especially need guidance and reinforcement if they are to be genuine resisters of war today. Some of the best individuals I have known in this world have never had the training or education to answer the sort of questions that seem to be bothering some of our own leaders. Those questions are genuine ones and should

bother many of us but until we ourselves have thought
them through nothing can be gained by pounding away at
them. All of them are ancient questions and have baffled
the best minds in history. Right now we are confronted by
a monstrous evil known as war by which I mean what the
man on the street understands by war—our present institution of massed violence and despotism. Nothing in our
practical life is more important than to destroy that institution. It will destroy us and the things we stand for if it
can't be ended. Surely that is enough for us right now.
That task is enormous and complex but it must be met.
Several of the best conscientious objectors I knew in the
last war have criticised the American pacifist movement
for the past twenty years because they felt it failed to
concentrate on the one means of ending war, viz., the
refusal to fight. . . . It is perfectly true that if we understand clearly we will realize that all of us are sinners and
we all are caught in a complex social net that makes all
of us take a more or less active part in social sins. But where
war is concerned we can do something to end that particular abomination. Since we can do something we should do
it. We can refuse to be conscripted and I know of nothing
more positive in its ultimate implications than that action
today. In later years other actions may be more important
though I doubt if the time will ever come when freedom
of conscience will not be one of the most important things
in life both for the individual and society.

I have no desire to urge any individual to become a
Conscientious Objector who is not convinced that such
action is right. I have no criticism of men who took non-
combatant service in the last war but I am glad there were
men who did not take it. I hope that some of the Fellowship Of Reconciliation youth will refuse similar non-
combatant service in the next war if there is one. That does
not mean that I will feel or think that those who take such
service are not doing their full duty. It merely means that

I hope some will go the whole way in resisting a conscription act in which I do not believe.

The youth that will count most in holding aloft the banner of freedom of conscience will be the ones who resist the evil of a conscription act for war all the way to jail or even to death. They won't be 100% consistent. None of us can be. We must face that fact but not to the point of failing to do what we can do.

The convictions here expressed I share to the full after having gone through the experience of being during the last war a preacher who would not "present arms" and who was compelled to resign from the pulpit of a Christian church on that account; and after having also gone through the experience of completely abandoning pacifism for a period of years and exploring with all the energy, intelligence, and sincerity of which I am capable other than non-violent ways for achieving a better world. Refusal of individual after individual to support any war or war preparation is the most positive, the most constructive, the most patriotic, the sanest, the most Christian social act men can perform today. Until people thus make it impossible for the nations, especially their own, to use war as a method for approaching any problem, men will not put their minds seriously to finding other ways to deal with situations. Unless war is abandoned, the light of democracy will be quenched in one land after another. Until war is abolished, the whole movement for social justice is halted.

It is true enough that with war rejected much else remains for mankind to do; but in the first place, nothing else can be done until this step of war-renunciation is taken, and in the second place, men have abundant means, once they awake from this nightmare and return from the realm of fantasy in which there is always "one more war" to end war that has to be fought to the realm of reality, with which to build a world. Verily, as Auden has said, "to matter entire, to the unbounded vigors of the instrument, to all logical precision," we are "the rejoicing heirs." We need not be too much troubled now by the question of what we have to do once we cease to be lured by "the immediate dividend" promised by hatred and trust in "disciplined love." Vast energies, material, human, spiritual, wait to go into action once we abandon war.

Under the circumstances to say that war-renunciation is negative and so by inference to condemn or belittle it is like suggesting that releasing the throttle and taking the brakes off a train, which with steam up and fully manned stands stock still at a switch while another train in the distance comes bearing down upon it, is a purely negative and unimportant matter. It is like saying that the physician who has checked a disease which, if unchecked, would have killed the patient, has done only a negative thing—after all, he has only stopped the sickness; but the point is that that having been done the great positive forces of life have their way and may be trusted to surge forward.

Chapter IX

The Church and the Revolution of Peace

IN THE CLOSING PARAGRAPHS OF THE PRECEDING CHAPTER WE HAVE INSISTED THAT WAR-RENUNCIATION IN ITSELF, especially on the part of citizens of the leading nations of the western world, may in a superficial sense be a negative action but is in essence a positive action bound to have constructively revolutionary consequences on all our social life. Nevertheless, our preoccupation in this book has not been with mere war-resistance or with a narrow and secular anti-war movement. Our concern has been with the problems and crisis of modern civilization as a whole; with the achievement of a dynamic, beautiful, and noble social order, the realization of the ancient prophetic dream of the Kingdom of God on earth. We have seen that the Communist movement, aiming at the realization of the prophetic ideal of justice, freedom, and brotherhood, has nevertheless become a force of evil rather than good, because it succumbed to the belief that evil can overcome evil, dictatorship is the road to democracy, violence the way to peace. Certainly such happenings as the Stalin-Hitler pact, the invasion of Poland and Finland, have furnished saddening corroboration of our analysis written long before these events occurred. We have not devoted any time to a similar analysis of the various forms of fascism simply because in western Europe and the United States this form of totalitarianism has never been widely regarded as a means of deliverance for our age. To sincere followers of Fascist and Nazi systems also, however, recent events must have been thoroughly disillusioning. A pact between nazism and communism, each of which justified its existence for many years as mankind's sole defence against the other, must produce upon devotees still capable of feeling and thought much the same reaction as a united front between the Roman Catholic church and the Russian "League of the Godless" might produce upon the members of these two organizations! In this respect the way has been made easier for alternative systems of life, economics, and government.

As the politicians, however, point out, "you cannot defeat somebody with nobody." If there is no clear alternative to the movement for social change by violence, men will continue to turn to bolshevism no matter how horrible its aspect may become. There must be something more than a vacuum to meet this force. Naturally we turn, therefore, to ask whether those movements which do not rely upon violence hold out real promise to mankind in its desperate crisis. This means the pacifist movement and the church, both of which claim that they seek a new world but by non-violent, pure, spiritual means. We must confess that neither the pacifist movement nor the churches nor both together seem adequate to the task. In more sober moments we are tempted to say that they seem almost hopelessly inadequate.

One of the chief reasons for this condition is that the pacifist movement has not yet made its reckoning with religion and that, on the other hand, the churches have not yet settled their account with pacifism, with the implications of non-violence in their own Scriptures and the most sacred doctrines they profess. Pacifism if it be not a mere opportunist political device, is religion, a view and a way of life, or it is nothing; and the pacifist movement has not yet adequately envisaged or acted upon that fact. Religion, Christianity is pacifism in the sense just indicated, is the way of love, of non-violence, of the Cross, or else it becomes a mockery, with no vital connection with the Jewish-Christian prophetic tradition, with Biblical revelation. The churches must become pacifist or in the present historical situation they will no longer be able to call themselves Christian. It is these ideas which we must develop in the remaining pages of this book.

We approach the matter in the first instance from the standpoint of the development that is needed in the pacifist movement. A fully effective pacifist movement must, we have suggested, rest on a religious foundation; a purely political anti-war movement will not meet the world's need even in the matter of abolishing international war. Violence is not a tool or instrument that one can pick up or lay down, use in this relationship of life but not in that other, use today and discard tomorrow. Violence is an approach to life, a way of life. Men, groups, nations, live and act in a certain way; then one day they find that a sword has grown in their hand, violence has become a part of their very being. Stopping war when such a situation arises requires indeed such a spiritual operation as Jesus prescribed when he said: "If your hand offends you, cut it off and cast it from you. It is better to go maimed into life, than having two hands to be cast into the hell of fire."

The basic thing the religious pacifist has in mind when he emphasizes the need of a religious basis for the pacifist movement is that pacifism also must be an inner experience, an inner attitude, a way of life, not merely a tool or device which the individual uses in certain circumstances on his environment. One must not only favor pacifism or non-violence as a policy in such and such circumstances, one must *be* a pacifist.

The issue here indicated is a deep-going one which has a bearing not merely on the problem of war but on the whole problem of building a sane, decent, and beautiful world. We have tended for some decades to think of that problem as almost exclusively one of changing outward arrangements, revolutionizing "the system," as a task in "social engineering." It is true that men cannot live a democratic life in a world that is autocratically organized —a fully Christian life in an economic and political order built on non-Christian or anti-Christian foundations. But the very extent and intensity of the crisis of our civilization has led many thinkers in recent years to realize that there is another side to the problem, viz., the question of the nature of man, the quality of the human being. One after another our movements of reform and revolution break down because the human material in them is not equal to the task; leaders and members do not develop the self-discipline, the integrity, the solidarity required for victory.

When the typical reformer or revolutionist proclaims

the new order, he goes on to urge men to "organize, agitate, get out the vote, fight." Jesus also proclaimed "The Kingdom of God, [i.e., the revolution] is at hand"; but immediately added in true prophetic fashion, "Repent." That is to say, if we are to have a new world, we must have new men; if you want a revolution, you must be revolutionized. A world of peace will not be achieved by men who in their own souls are torn with strife and eagerness to assert themselves. In the degree that the anti-war or pacifist movement is composed of individuals who have not themselves, to use Aldous Huxley's phrase, achieved "detachment," who have not undergone an inner revolution, it too will experience the same failure to achieve self-discipline, integrity, true fellowship among its own members which has afflicted other movements for social change. Who indeed would be so bold as to say that our pacifist organizations have not suffered from such things?

Let us note in passing that what holds good of the relation between inner and outer revolution holds good also of the relationship of means and ends. Pacifists all know how to laugh—perhaps a little too gleefully—at the man who thinks the way to end war is by one more "really good" war. But are we free, for example, from the notion that pacifism may be promoted, or at any rate, war abolished, by those high-pressure methods such as beating down opponents in an argument, which in principle involve the same kind of violation of personality as war itself?

What the religious pacifist is, then, trying to say is that only in the degree that men are at peace within, are themselves subjected to the spirit of peace and love, and use only the methods of constructive good-will, can they work effectively for pacifism.

Two other things are implied in the position of religious pacifism which we simply mention without amplification. The first is that pacifism implies and is rooted in one's conviction about ultimate reality, the universe, God; the conviction that this reality is fellowship, love, that man is the creation, the child of this reality, and the human family is therefore in the profoundest sense one; "the neighbor" is my "other self" and I can therefore no more think of wanting to put him in the wrong, to outwit him, to injure or destroy him than I can think of wanting to do these things to myself. The second is that there are in our universe resources for living the life of love which we have hardly begun to tap, but which we must learn to draw upon.

Now the question as to whether such religious pacifism is the "true" pacifism, which alone can be expected to prove effective, is by far the most important question confronting the pacifist forces, and for that matter all ethical and religious and progressive forces in our day. We desperately need to know what is the sound way to meet our crisis; we can ill afford to be mistaken in the matter!

The religious or Christian pacifist cannot keep from proclaiming his conviction, his "gospel." Being a religious or Christian pacifist means precisely to be possessed by this conviction, to have not only one's mind but one's whole being held in its grip. Furthermore, in the nature of the case the experience has brought him a personal release, "salvation," which he cannot help, literally or figuratively, singing aloud.

It is true that there are those who think of themselves as Christian pacifists who have, or give the impression of having, an attitude of superiority, even perhaps of exclusiveness or arrogance toward others. In the degree that such an attitude characterizes any of us, we are not yet Christian pacifists. This attitude is the denial of fellowship. In so far as we are truly religious pacifists we are aware of our oneness with all our fellows, and of our own unfaithfulness to love—aware that we are the liar, the thief, the prostitute, the war-maker, the dictator, the man or woman constantly falling short of a full expression of love.

Of course, too, this is not a matter of adopting this or that dogmatic formulation of religious pacifism, nor of verbal profession. It is not a question of saying "Lord, Lord," but of "doing the will" of God. There are those who deny being religious pacifists who are just that, as there are those who say they are religious pacifists who are nothing of the sort.

But on the essence of the matter, there can be, it seems to me, no equivocation. If we hold the religious pacifist position we must necessarily assert its centrality. We shall be profoundly convinced that the core of any effective movement against war must be composed of those who by the grace of God and a genuine religious experience have put the spirit of domination and strife out of their own hearts, and therefore are able to help banish them from the various relationships of life; it must be composed of those who really believe in the overcoming power of prayer and humility and sacrifice. This does not mean that we cannot work whole-heartedly on many things with those in the churches or in the general peace movement who do not share our faith. But in any such organizations we must necessarily be a distinctive force and must proclaim the faith that is in us. Not, be it said, by getting up as often as possible to recite our credo! Rather first of all precisely by showing in these organizations the spirit of humility, respect for personality, self-effacement, constructive good-will. In turn, the members of these organizations cannot evade the responsibility of asking whether their impatience at the assertion that religious pacifism is the "truth" is due to the arrogance with which that statement is sometimes made, or to their own failure really to face up to and think through the issue involved.

There remain two matters in this general field on which a very brief comment must suffice. One is the matter of doctrine, theology, philosophy. No living movement can get along without them. This goes for religious pacifism. Rejection of theology or philosophy is also theology or philosophy. We shall be aided in maintaining fellowship in the midst of differences in this field by remembering, first, that theology is not basic but life; second, that theology always has been and is now a developing thing, and that we certainly greatly need a restatement of our basic faith in the language and thought-form of our own day; third, that no theologizing or philosophizing about love can be sound unless it is pursued in the spirit of love and not of divisiveness.

The other question is that of terminology, symbols and worship. When we deal with ultimate things, with God, we all necessarily speak in symbols, in the language of poetry, using different art-forms as it were, in order to express and lay hold on the Ineffable. A symbol that means much to one may mean nothing to another; a symbol that conveys precious truth and emotion to one may repel another. Because human beings must necessarily seek to convey thought and feeling through some language, not equally understood or loved by all, and since it is not possible to manufacture symbols to order in a hurry, an organization may at a given point in its development minister most effectively to those who speak in certain symbols. In one sense this may mean limitation, yet in another sense greater effectiveness.

The problem cannot be solved by underestimating the rôle of symbols. There is nothing wise or "broad" about not trying to talk to folk in "their own language." Neither is the difficulty met by talking exclusively in abstract, technical language which bears no freight of emotion. No movement of any sort, and certainly no religious one, can "move" if it becomes thus over-intellectualized.

There is a unity underlying all differences. In "the silence" we find it together. As we worship and above all toil and sacrifice together, we shall find ways to express in words and in other symbols what the Eternal Love reveals to us in that silence. In part this may mean finding new words and symbols; in part it may well be by putting new meaning into old symbols, as has happened in the spiritual history of the race, and as a result of which symbols and forms that once seemed divisive unite men not only with their contemporaries but with the generations gone before, who also communed with the Eternal Love at the heart of all and sought to express what they thus learned within the limits of human speech and symbolic act.

It will be impossible for individuals to whom this revolutionary inner experience of the nature of life and the universe has come to remain isolated individuals warming their own hands at this inner glow or to be content with belonging to what might be called pacifist or anti-war clubs, organizations which impose no genuine discipline upon their members and which have no serious program of action. On the contrary, the very experience which such persons have had of the love or fellowship which is at the heart of all things will, on the one hand, draw them to those who have had a like experience and, on the other hand, lead them to desire to forge an instrument of which they are a part and which is part of their own being, so that the Kingdom of God may be brought in, the revolution, of which they have envisaged the possibility, may be achieved. They will inevitably join or seek to form, if they do not seem to find it in existence, what corresponds to the Christian's idea of the True, Universal Church or the Leninist's idea of The Party or The Internationale.

Now this problem of the instrument for the realization of the hopes of man, the prophetic vision, is so important not only for the pacifist believer in "the revolution of peace," but for the entire movement for social justice, for the Christian and Jewish churches, for this age in which we live, that we must take the time to analyze it further. It is significant that it is precisely this problem which seems to enlist the interest of thinkers in all social movements today. We cannot go on as we are. The great deliverance must come. But how? Where is The Party? Where is the True Church? Among pacifists, the increasing preoccupation with what are variously called pacifist cells, peace teams, pacifist action fellowships, for the three-fold purpose of worship, study, and action, is illustrative of the point. Lenin, it is interesting to note, was really concerned about two things: the nature and structure of a revolutionary party, and how the party might acquire state power. The great split of the Russian social democratic movement into Bolshevik and Menshevik wings was not over a great philosophical or economic issue, but over the question of a highly centralized party such as Lenin was determined to have versus a decentralized, "democratic" party such as the Mensheviks wanted. It is a patent fact that in the Fascist or Nazi, as in the Bolshevik, scheme the idea and the fact of The Party are all-important. Are not Christian circles rediscovering the "church"?

Let us return for a moment to Lenin. It is astonishing how many of the marks of the True Church or of a world-wide fellowship to achieve "the revolution of peace" are included in his doctrine of The Party. The Party must be revolutionary. The existing order is corrupt; it is also unable any longer to function; it is doomed. The Party must therefore aim to replace it, not to come to an understanding with it. The Party stands over against "the world," therefore. It is despised, it is weak, it is in a hopeless minority, it is misunderstood, it is outrageously persecuted—until the day of revolution dawns. Then when the more imposing and less intransigent parties stand paralyzed before a world falling to pieces, The Party will fill the breach.

The Party is the instrument of God—of destiny, at any rate, of those "historical forces which make the triumph of socialism inevitable." A force which makes for the reign of righteousness and brotherhood, to which the individual

must surrender himself utterly, and which cannot fail—
that comes close to being a definition of, let us say, a
Calvinist God. The Party accordingly cannot really fail.
"Fear not, little flock." It has the deposit of the truth.
It cannot do wrong, since at a given moment nothing can
be nearer right than the instrument of historic destiny.

There can on these terms be only one true party. The
individual member, if he be a true member who has no
will but The Party's will, will find ineffable joy in its
service. Without The Party, the proletariat is lost. Of
itself, through its own experience, without being led by
The Party, it will not rise to revolutionary heights and be
able to save itself. "The basic error," Lenin wrote, "is the
idea that political consciousness can be developed in the
workers from within. . . . Political consciousness can only
be impressed on the workers from outside," and through
The Party, of the elite, the elect, through the "ecclesia."

The Party, Lenin contended, must be international, universal, in scope and in essence. Violently he contended
against the leaders of the Second Internationale who
thought in terms of a British, Dutch, German, Russian
party affiliated to the Internationale. There could be only
one Internationale with British, Dutch, and so forth sections, but sections without autonomy. "One, holy catholic church," a world-wide fellowship. When finally The
Party triumphs, history as we know it comes to an end,
or rather history begins for the first time. Man will pass,
in Engels' great phrase, "from the kingdom of necessity
into the kingdom of freedom."

It was, my masters, a magnificent attempt to sketch and
to create the True Church for which men long, and be-

cause of its daring and its partial truth and because of the apostasy of Christ's church, not least in Russia itself, it was given to Lenin's church to have power for a season, and to win many devout adherents, and to be the midwife for the "historical forces" in one of the great hours in human history—and Lenin has become an ikon.

Why is Lenin's party failing, and why can we not accept it as the true church, the fellowship of those on whom the coming of history's new day indeed depends? Of the many things that need to be said in answer to that question, I must confine myself to mentioning two. For one thing, Lenin rightly discerned that if you are to exercise control over the flux of the historical present, you must believe that you have a position outside and above it; and that if you are to have the strength and the courage to break down the pillars of this temple and in three days to build another in which the goal of all history will be achieved, then you must be in league with destiny itself. But this, as I have already suggested, is to speak of God, the true God, the Almighty. Then, as Lenin did, you have to wage relentless war against all those you regard as false gods, which for Lenin meant above all against Christ. But then, also, the question is obviously raised: Is your God verily God? And just as in the case of the human being the question as to whether he is "really" human has to do with his character, so the ultimate question about your God has to do with His character.

This leads to a second and closely related question. If you have The Party which is international, universal, the depository of the truth, the sole instrument for the redemption of mankind, without which there is no salvation, which can brook no rivals, since to do so would be to deny its divine commission and to turn mankind over to destruction—and this party is composed of human beings, albeit "the elect"—how can you prevent such a party from becoming the instrument of unspeakable pride and tyranny and hence tearing itself to pieces? Obviously you cannot, and your advice to the inner circle of your party, "Don't make the mistake the leaders of the French Revolution made and get to killing each other off," will go unheeded, if you begin, as Lenin did, by assuming that the character of its members, save in the one respect of self-effacement for The Party, is not of first-rate importance and that the party may employ any means in order to achieve its end.

The positive phase of the answer to this most crucial question about the international party or the Universal Church is stated in the classic chapter on Karl Marx in J. Middleton Murry's recent *Heroes of Thought*:

"To keep alive within any human society the sense of the reality of Good and Evil as absolutes, independent of the convention of the society, or the ordinance of the secular state, is the function of a church . . . Therefore the institution of the church is precious, but precious only in so far as it asserts and justifies in act the claim to possess an authority superior to that of the secular state, because derived from its knowledge of the absolute Good, which is God. . . . Further, it is self-evident that there is but one safeguard against the abuse of this authority of the church, namely, that the absolute Good in obedience to which its authority consists should forbid persecution, and command nonresistance to evil. This the God of the invisible Christian church does command."

Without a fellowship of those who have found the truth, who are in league with the universe, with the very heart of reality, who have surrendered themselves to the good and find all their joy in its service, who have taken up the Cross and are ready to lose their life so that they may find it; a fellowship which knows no bounds but is universal in character and intention; a fellowship of hope and faith which as all that men have relied on goes to pieces knows that thus the way is opened for a better order, that "the Kingdom of God is at hand"—without such a fellowship mankind is lost. It is, to use figures that Jesus employed, like meat with no salt to keep it from putrefying; like a room without a candle; like a dull lump of dough with no yeast to set it fermenting with new life. But such a fellowship of those who believe that they are chosen of God to bring in his Kingdom, that they are the instruments of destiny whom no one and nothing will be able to stop or should be permitted to stop, such a church, such a party is always in danger of becoming a supreme instrument of tyranny, as the history of churches and parties has so often illustrated. There is terrific power in complete surrender of the self to an idea; such a self becomes indeed an agent of elemental forces. But those forces may be demonic as well as divine. The fellowship, the church, the party of "the elect" will indeed save and redeem men and advance the genuine fulfillment of human history only if the reality, the God, from whom the dedicated draw their strength is love, and if the only means by